PHILADELPHIA
USA

PHILADELPHIA USA

ROBERT H. WILSON

PHOTOGRAPHS BY CHARLES P. MILLS

DESIGN BY RAYMOND A. BALLINGER

PUBLISHED BY CHILTON BOOK COMPANY

SPONSORED BY GIRARD BANK

AN OFFICIAL PHILADELPHIA '76 BICENTENNIAL PUBLICATION

Philadelphia '76, Incorporated is the official agency
for coordinating observance of the 1776 Bicentennial in Philadelphia,
the birthplace of the United States.
The Corporation extends its sincere thanks to
Girard Bank, of Philadelphia, which has sponsored the
publication of this volume as one of its Bicentennial projects.

Copyright © 1975 by Robert H. Wilson
First Edition   All Rights Reserved
Published in Radnor, Pennsylvania, by Chilton Book Company
and simultaneously in Don Mills, Ontario, Canada,
by Thomas Nelson & Sons, Ltd.
Library of Congress Catalog Card Number 75-7554
ISBN: 0-8019-6299-4 Cloth Edition
ISBN: 0-8019-6300-1 Paper Edition
Manufactured in the United States of America

2 3 4 5 6 7 8 9 0   4 3 2 1 0 9 8 7 6 5

Typesetting by John C. Meyer & Son, Inc.
Printing by Smith-Edwards-Dunlap Company
Binding by Haddon Bindery

Philadelphia, a great modern city, is a metropolis of widely diverse commerce, industry and finance; and it is one of the world's major seaports. A center of education, medicine, law, music, fine arts and religion, it is also a livable city of comfortable homes and convenient transportation. But Philadelphia is best known as a city of history. William Penn granted Philadelphians religious freedom and self-government nearly a century before 1776. Benjamin Franklin, the most famous man in colonial America, lived and worked here. In Philadelphia, independence was declared, the United States of America was born and George Washington served as first President. The attractiveness of twentieth century Philadelphia is the way the old, historic city has been carefully preserved in the midst of the modern as seen in this view from the visitors' center at the top of Penn Mutual Tower on Independence Square.

Philadelphie, grande métropole moderne, est aussi bien la ville la plus historique des Etats-Unis. L'ancienne ville est soigneusement préservée en plein milieu de la nouvelle, comme on peut voir sur cette prise de vue d'en haut de la Penn Mutual Tower, Independance Square.

Philadelphia, eine moderne Weltstadt, ist, historisch gesehen, die bedeutendste Stadt Amerikas. Die Altstadt, von neuen Bauten umgeben, ist gut erhalten, wie das folgende Bild zeigt (Blick vom Penn Mutual Tower auf dem Independence Square).

Philadelphia, una gran metrópoli moderna, es también la ciudad más histórica de América. La ciudad vieja está cuidadosamente preservada en medio de todo lo nuevo, como se ve en esta vista desde la Penn Mutual Tower en Independence Square.

William Penn's Quaker "Experiment"

Philadelphia was founded in 1681 by William Penn, an English Quaker. Penn received a grant of 26,000,000 acres from King Charles II who named the Province "Pennsylvania". For the principal settlement, Penn chose the Biblical name "Philadelphia"—meaning "City of Brotherly Love".

A huge statue of "Billy Penn" at the top of City Hall tower is Philadelphia's best known landmark. By common consent, but not as a matter of law, no building in the city rises higher than the base of the Founder's statue.

The tower statue, erected in 1894, was modeled after one executed a century before in England which was presented to Pennsylvania Hospital by Penn's grandson and now stands in the yard of the hospital at Eighth and Spruce Streets. In the left hand is shown the historic 1701 Charter of Liberties in which Penn granted his colonists religious and political freedom. The original charter is preserved at the American Philosophical Society.

Philadelphie fut fondée en 1681 par le Quaker anglais, William Penn qui était propriétaire de l'entière province de Pennsylvanie. Une énorme statue de Penn située en haut de l'Hôtel de ville est le monument le mieux connu de la ville. Une autre statue, plus ancienne, dans Pennsylvania Hospital représente Penn qui tient à la main sa célèbre Charte de Libertés de 1701.

Philadelphia wurde 1681 von dem englischen Quäker William Penn gegründet, dem Verwalter der ganzen Provinz von Pennsylvania. Eine grosse Statue von Penn, die auf dem Rathausturm steht, ist die bekannteste Sehenswürdigkeit der Stadt. Eine ältere Statue auf den Geländen des Pennsylvania Hospitals zeigt Penn mit dem historischen Charter of Liberties von 1701 in der Hand.

Philadelphia fue fundada en 1681 por el cuáquero inglés William Penn, quien fue propietario de la provincia entera de Pennsylvania. Una estatua enorme de Penn encima de la torre del Ayuntamiento es la mejor marca de la ciudad. Una estatua más antigua en Pennsylvania Hospital muestra a Penn con su histórica Cédula de Libertades de 1701 en la mano.

Unlike earlier colonists in Virginia and Massachusetts who struggled to build homes in the wilderness, those who came to Philadelphia in 1681 were purchasers of lots in a well planned community. Before any left Europe, Penn's surveyor had laid out the city in a checkerboard of straight streets and open park spaces.

The original plan is still the design of modern Philadelphia. City Hall stands in the Center Square, which is named for Penn himself. The other four squares still exist, named for Franklin, Washington, David Rittenhouse and James Logan. This is Logan Square, northwest of City Hall.

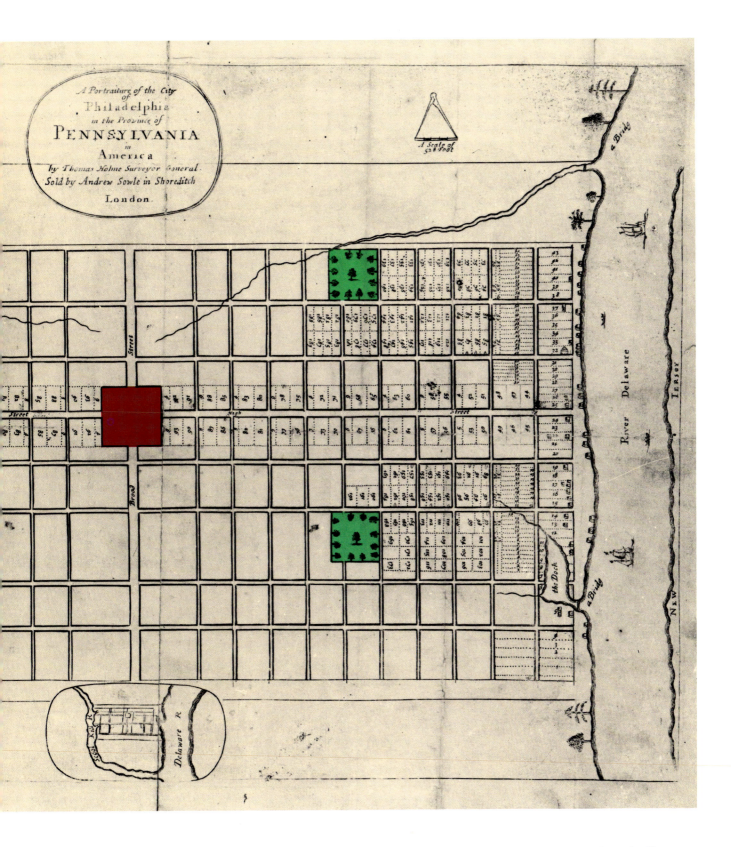

L'arpenteur de Penn avait disposé d'un plan total de Philadelphie avant le peuplement de la ville. Les rues et les terrains des parcs originaux existent toujours. Voici Logan Square, situé au nord-ouest de l'Hôtel de ville.

Penns Landmesser zeichneten den vollständigen Plan von Philadelphia, ehe die ersten Ansiedler ankamen. Die ursprünglichen Strassen und Parkanlagen existieren heute noch. Das Bild zeigt Logan Square, nordwestlich von dem Rathaus.

El agrimensor de Penn le dispuso un plan completo de Philadelphia antes de la llegada de los pobladores. Todavía existen las calles originales y los espacios para parques. Todo esto es Logan Square, al noroeste del Ayuntamiento.

The stately government building begun in 1732 for the Province of Pennsylvania is occasionally called The State House by some Philadelphians, but most of the world now knows it as Independence Hall.

Meeting here in 1751, the Provincial Assembly voted to purchase a 2,000 pound bell for the tower then being added to the building. The year 1751 was a jubilee year—the 50th anniversary of the Charter of Liberties granted by Penn in 1701. A scholarly committeeman delegated to choose an appropriate inscription for the bell turned to the Old Testament Book of Leviticus. Chapter 25, Verse 10, referring to ancient Hebrew tradition of freeing bondmen in jubilee years, begins: "And ye shall hallow the fiftieth year, and proclaim liberty throughout all the land unto all the inhabitants thereof." The concluding words became the first line of the inscription. The second line read: "By order of the Assembly of the Province of Pensylvania for the State House in Philada."

The bell was made in England, arrived in Philadelphia in 1752 and cracked while being tested after a rough ocean crossing. The "Ingenious Work-men", Pass and Stow, recast it; and beginning in 1753, its booming tone was heard throughout Colonial Philadelphia.

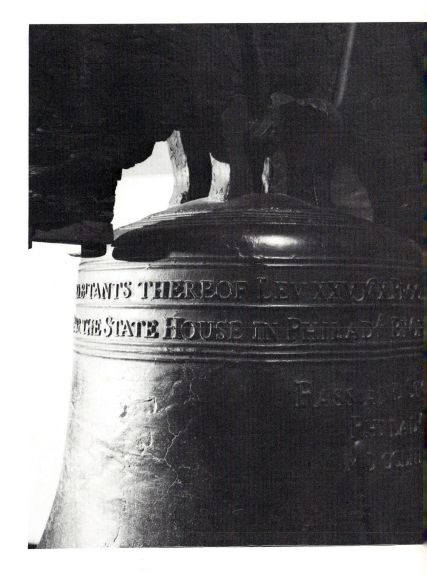

On the second floor of the State House, the Governor's Council Chamber was the executive office of the colonial Province and, later, the early State of Pennsylvania.

In 1698, Old Swedes' Church (Gloria Dei) was built just to the south of Philadelphia by Swedish settlers who had lived along the Delaware for half a century before Penn became Proprietor. This building replaced a log structure which had served both as blockhouse and place of worship.

Penn insisted that his Province be "an Holy Experiment" where all people—not just Quakers—could worship God as they chose. Members of the Swedish church, originally Lutheran, eventually united with the Church of England, and Gloria Dei is now an active Episcopal parish with services every Sunday.

Penn déclara sa Province "une Sainte Expérience" où tous—non pas les Quakers seuls—pourraient adorer Dieu comme bon leur semblait. Voici Old Swedes' Church (Gloria Dei) construite en 1698-1700, située un peu au sud des bornes de l'ancienne ville de Philadelphie. C'est une église en pleine activité où les services religieux ont lieu tous les dimanches.

Penn erklärte seine Provinz als "ein heiliges Experiment," in der alle Menschen, nicht nur die Quäker, vollständige Glaubensfreiheit geniessen könnten. Das Bild zeigt Old Swedes' Church (Gloria Dei), erbaut 1698-1700 ausserhalb der südlichen Stadtgrenze Philadelphias. In dieser Kirche wird heute noch jeden Sonntag der Gottesdienst gehalten.

Penn nombró su Provincia un "Experimento Sagrado" donde toda la gente— no solamente los cuáqueros—pudiera venerar a Dios como prefirieron. Esta es la iglesia Old Swedes' (Gloria Dei) edificada en 1698-1700 justamente al sur de la frontera de la ciudad de Philadelphia. Es todavía una iglesia activa con servicios todos los domingos.

Au premier étage de la Chambre de l'Etat on trouve la Salle du Conseil du Gouverneur qui fut le lieu du pouvoir exécutif de la province coloniale et, plus tard, du nouvel état de Pennsylvanie.

Im ersten Stock des State House war die Beratungskammer des Gouverneurs das Verwaltungsamt der kolonialen Provinz und später des jungen Staates von Pennsylvania.

En el segundo piso de la Casa de Estado, la Cámara de Consejo del Gobernador fue el despacho ejecutivo de la provincia colonial y, más tarde, del nuevo estado de Pennsylvania.

The earliest Quaker meeting houses in Philadelphia were eventually replaced by newer and larger structures such as the ample brick Arch Street Meeting near Fourth Street. It was built in 1804 on land which William Penn had originally deeded in 1693 for a burial ground. Every spring, the Philadelphia Yearly Meeting of the Religious Society of Friends is held here.

Of the original meeting houses in Penn's province, the oldest survivor is that of Merion Meeting. It was erected in 1695 by Welsh Quakers who settled on a large tract west of the city. Penn himself once spoke here at a Meeting for Worship in the same plain little room in which services are still held every Sunday, or First Day.

On a remplacé les premiers temples des Quakers à Philadelphie avec d'autres plus grands tels que le temple Arch Street Meeting, construit en 1804. Le plus ancien des temples originaux est Merion Meeting construit en 1695 par des Quakers du pays de Galles qui s'installèrent à l'ouest de Philadelphie.

Die ältesten Gemeindehäuser der Quäker in Philadelphia, wie das Gemeindehaus an der Archstrasse, das im Jahre 1804 erbaut wurde, wurden durch neuere und grössere ersetzt. Das älteste der Originalgebäude ist das Merion Meeting, das 1695 von Quäkern aus Wales gebaut wurde, die sich westlich von Philadelphia niederliessen.

Las más antiguas casas de asamblea de los cuáqueros fueron substituidas por unas más modernas y más grandes como la amplia casa de piedra en la Calle Arch construída en 1804. La más antigua de las originales casas de Asamblea es Merion Meeting, edificada en 1695 por los cuáqueros galos quienes poblaron las secciones al oeste de Philadelphia.

Colonists of many different religious groups followed the Quakers to Philadelphia and established houses of worship which still exist in the modern city.

A Jesuit priest built St. Joseph's Church near Fourth and Walnut Streets in 1733 at a time when the laws of Great Britain forbad celebration of Catholic Mass elsewhere in the English world. The church has been rebuilt, but the entry-way from Willings Alley is reminiscent of colonial days.

The Penn family in 1738 sold to Nathan Levy the lot on Spruce Street near Eighth which became the burial ground of Mikveh Israel, the first Jewish congregation. It was not until after the Revolution that the congregation built its first synagogue. Now it plans to build a new one on Independence Mall.

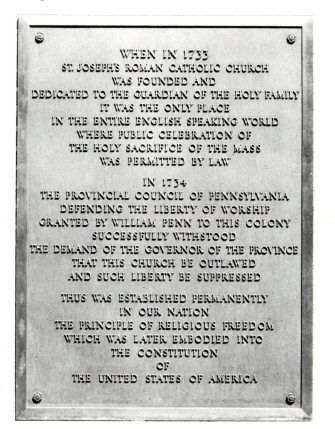

Des colons de nombreuses religions suivirent les Quakers à Philadelphie. En 1738 la famille Penn fournit le terrain qui devint le cimetière de Mikveh Israel, une assemblée juive. Un jésuite fit bâtir l'Eglise St. Joseph en 1733 quand la messe catholique fut interdite partout dans le monde de langue anglaise.

Kolonisten verschiedener Glaubensbekennung folgten den Quäkern nach Philadelphia. 1738 stellte die Familie Penn den jüdischen Bewohnern der Stadt ein Grundstück zur Verfügung, das zum Friedhof der Gemeinde Mikveh Israel wurde. Ein Jesuitenpater erbaute im Jahre 1733, als die katholische Messe in der ganzen englisch-sprechenden Welt verboten war, die St. Joseph's Church.

Los colonos de muchas diferentes creencias religiosas siguieron a los cuáqueros a Philadelphia. En 1738 la familia de Penn proporcionó terrenos que llegaron a ser el cementerio de la congregación judaica, Mikveh Israel. Un cura jesuita construyó la iglesia Saint Joseph en 1733 cuando se prohibió la misa católica por todo el resto del mundo de habla inglesa.

The Colonial City of Benjamin Franklin

Elfreth's Alley remains much as it was when Philadelphia was the leading city of the thirteen colonies. Near Second and Arch Streets, surrounded by a busy commercial neighborhood, it is still a quiet place of private residences.

In 1723, at the nearby riverfront, Benjamin Franklin first landed in Philadelphia. His *Autobiography* tells how he walked along just such streets as this, a hungry 17-year-old printer looking for work. The statue portraying his arrival stands in front of Franklin Field, the athletic stadium of the University of Pennsylvania.

Five years after his arrival, Franklin began his own printing business. The next year he bought out a one-year-old newspaper and built it into the largest in the colonies. At 27, he began publishing *Poor Richard's Almanack*. He earned a fortune by the time he was 40, and lived to 84—scholar, scientist, diplomat, statesman and Philadelphia's greatest citizen.

Elfreth's Alley près des rues 2 et Arch, reste à peu près telle qu'elle était en 1723 quand le jeune Benjamin Franklin arriva, cherchant du travail d'imprimeur. La statue de cette arrivée se trouve sur le campus de l'Université de Pennsylvanie.

Elfreth's Alley, in der Nähe von der Second— und der Archstrasse, bleibt heute noch wie sie 1723 war, als der junge Benjamin Franklin in die Stadt kam, um Arbeit als Buckdrucker zu suchen. Zur Erinnerung an seine Ankunft in Philadelphia wurde auf dem Gelände der University of Pennsylvania eine Statue von ihm errichtet.

Elfreth's Alley, cerca de las Calles Second y Arch, mantiene casi las mismas características de 1723 cuando llegó Benjamin Franklin buscando trabajo como impresor. Se puede ver la estatua de él conmemorando el día de su llegada en el claustro de la Universidad de Pennsylvania.

William Rittenhouse, one of Penn's early settlers, set up the first paper mill in America in 1690 on the bank of Wissahickon Creek. In 1707 he built this little house nearby, and it is still here although auto traffic now speeds quite close to the door. In this house David Rittenhouse, mathematician and astronomer, was born in 1732. He became a friend of Franklin and was director of the first United States mint. Rittenhouse Square is named for him.

Ce sont les maisons de deux grands hommes de Philadelphie coloniale. David Rittenhouse, astronome, naquit en 1707 dans la petite maison près de Wissahickon Creek. James Logan fit construire son élégante résidence, Stenton en 1728. Toutes les deux maisons appartiennent actuellement à la Ville.

Das sind die Häuser von zwei grossen Männern aus Philadelphias Kolonialzeit. David Rittenhouse, Astronom, wurde 1707 in einem kleinen Haus in der Nähe von Wissahickon Creek geboren; James Logan baute sein elegantes Haus, Stenton, im Jahre 1728. Beide Häuser sind jetzt im Besitz der Stadt Philadelphia.

Estás son las casas de dos hombres grandes de Filadelfia colonial. David Rittenhouse, un astrónomo, nacido en 1707, en la casa pequeña cerca riachuelo Wissahickon. James Logan construido su residencia elegante Stenton, en 1728. Ahora, ambos casas estan poseada por la ciudad de Filadelfia.

One of the largest of Philadelphia's colonial mansions—still in its unaltered form—is Stenton, the fine brick home built by James Logan in 1728. Originally it stood in a wooded, 500 acre tract well north of the city. Its separate back kitchen and its large stone barn are still intact.

James Logan first came to Philadelphia as William Penn's secretary at the age of 25. He became agent and spokesman for the Proprietor and his family in Pennsylvania, an able administrator of public affairs and a successful businessman in his own right. He was in his fifties when he built this lovely house now owned by the city, furnished and maintained by the National Society of the Colonial Dames of America in the Commonwealth of Pennsylvania. Here the scholarly Logan assembled a collection of classical and scientific books which surpassed all the personal or college libraries in colonial America. He left it to the people of Philadelphia.

Le jeune James Logan vint à Philadelphie pour la première fois en qualité de secrétaire à William Penn. Plus tard il devint administrateur et porte-parole pour la famille Penn dans Pennsylvania et aussi un homme d'affaires accompli. Il fit construire cette belle maison après avoir passé la cinquantaine. C'est ici qu'il assembla la meilleure bibliothèque de l'Amerique coloniale.

Der junge James Logan kam zum ersten Mal nach Philadelphia als William Penns Sekretär. Später wirkte er als Verwaltungsbeamter und vertrat die Rechte der Familie Penn in Pennsylvania. Er war auch ein erfolgreicher Geschäftsmann. Mit etwa 50 Jahren liess er dieses schöne Haus bauen, wo er die beste Bibliothek in kolonialem Amerika zusammenstellte.

James Logan vino por la primera vez a Philadelphia como un joven secretario de William Penn. Más tarde, fue administrador y portavoz por la familia de Penn en Pennsylvania tanto como un próspero hombre de negocios. Edificó esta hermosa casa cuand tenía unos cincuenta años, y aquí recogió la más importante biblioteca de la América colonial.

Gardens, tree-lined streets and hundreds of original colonial homes keep Philadelphia as Penn wanted it: "a greene Country Towne."

Des jardins, des rues bordées d'arbres, des centaines de maisons style colonial préservent la ville de Philadelphie telle que Penn l'avait conçue: "un bourg vert."

Gärten, Strassen von Bäumen umgeben, und hunderte von ursprünglichen Kolonialbauten erhalten Philadelphia, so wie es Penn wollte: "eine grüne Landstadt".

Jardines, calles con árboles, y centenares de originales casas coloniales mantienen a Philadelphia como Penn la prefería: "un pueblo campestre y verde".

Streets and houses of eighteenth-century Philadelphia help create a unique style of city life for twentieth-century residents.

Les rues et les maisons du dix-huitième siècle créent à Philadelphie un unique train de vie urbaine pour les habitants du vingtième siècle.

Strassen und Häuser aus dem Philadelphia des 18. Jahrhunderts tragen zum einzigartigen Stil des Stadtlebens der Bürger des 20. Jahrhunderts bei.

Las calles y las casas de Philadelphia de estilo del siglo diez y ocho crean estilo un unico en la vida ciudadana de los habitantes del siglo veinte.

The occupants of these tiny houses on Third Street near Pine take pride in maintaining them in the fashion of the year they were built—1771. This is less than a mile from the busiest corner of downtown Philadelphia.

Les habitants de ces petites maisons dans la 3ème rue près de la rue Pine sont fiers d'entretenir leurs domiciles à la manière de l'époque où elles furent construites—1771.

Die Bewohner dieser kleinen Häuser in der Thirdstrasse in der Nähe von der Pinestrasse sind stolz auf ihre Wohnungen und erhalten sie im Geiste der Zeit, in der sie gebaut worden sind (1771).

Los dueños de estas pequeñas casas de la Calle Third cerca de Pine son muy orgullosos de estas propiedades y las mantienen según el estilo del año de su construcción—1771.

In a home built in 1759 on Spruce Street near Second, the original kitchen with its deep fireplace has been made into an exquisite overnight guest room. Cooking for the present owners of this fine town house is done in a modern kitchen elsewhere in the house.

Une maison datant de 1759 dans la rue Spruce près de la 2ème rue où on peut voir la cuisine originale transformée en chambre d'ami.

In einem aus 1759 stammenden Haus in der Sprucestrasse in der Nähe von der Secondstrasse wurde die ursprüngliche Küche in ein entzückendes Gastzimmer umgebaut.

En una casa de 1759 en la Salle Spruce cerca de Second, se ha transformado la cocina en una exquisita casa de huéspedes.

On petition of Philadelphia members of the Church of England, a minister was sent in 1695, and the first Anglican church was built on Second Street near Market. Queen Anne, of England, sent a 1708 silver communion service which is still used on special occasions.

The original church was soon outgrown so in 1727 Christ Church began the large Georgian edifice which is still in service. Still displayed on its east wall, over the Palladian window, is a medallion with the head of King George II who was on the throne when the building was completed.

Christ Church became the fashionable church in early Philadelphia. Its membership included Franklin, Washington and many other historic figures. Seven signers of the Declaration of Independence are buried either in the churchyard itself or in the burial ground which the church established at Fifth and Arch Streets, then the far edge of the city.

Christ Church fut fondée en 1695. Ce grand édifice, style des rois Georges d'Angleterre, fut construit en 1727. L'église, actuellement en état de servir, utilise le service en argent présenté en cadeau par la reine Anne, et fait voir encore le médaillon-portrait du roi Georges II. Parmi ceux qui mirent leur signature à la Déclaration de l'Indépendance il y en a sept qui sont enterrés dans le cimetière dans la 2ème rue près de la rue Market ou bien dans l'autre au coin des rues 5 et Arch.

Die Christ Church, gegründet 1695, erbaute im Jahre 1727 dieses grosse Gebäude im georgianischen Stil. Es wird noch immer gebraucht, und das Silberservice, ein Geschenk der Königin Anne, wird noch immer benutzt. Die Ostwand des Gebäudes zeigt heute noch ein Bildnis von Georg II., König von England. Sieben Unterzeichner der Unabhängigkeits-erklärung liegen im Kirchhof (Secondstrasse in der Nähe der Marketstrasse) begraben oder auf dem Friedhof an der Ecke von der Fifth- und der Archstrasse.

La congregación de Christ Church, fundada en 1695, con-struyó este gran edificio georgiano en 1727. Todavía tiene servicios, todavía se usa el juego de plata regalado por la Reina Ana, y todavía expone en la pared del este el retrato de Jorge II de Inglaterra. Unos siete firmantes de la Declaración de Independencia están enterrados en el cemen-terio de la parroquia, Calle Second cerca de Market, o en el cementerio en las Calles Fifth y Arch.

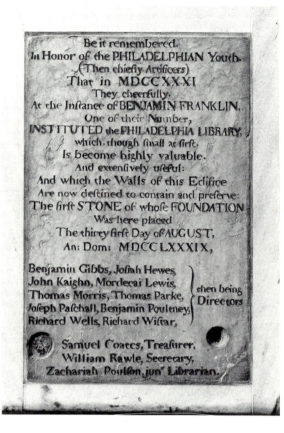

Young Benjamin Franklin persuaded fifty of his friends to form The Library Company of Philadelphia in 1731. It was a club whose members pooled dues to purchase books in England. For half a century the Library rented space, but the year before Franklin died it was able to put up its own building on Fifth Street. Franklin wrote the inscription for the cornerstone and lived to see the building completed in 1789. But he died before the statue of him was erected over the doorway. A William Birch print of 1800 shows the Library as it was then.

The Library Company moved in the 1880s, and its original building was torn down to make room for an office building. Now, that process has been reversed, and the office building has been demolished. On the same spot, and in the same architectural style as Franklin's building, there now stands the Library of the American Philosophical Society.

As for The Library Company of Philadelphia, now nearly 250 years old, it is still thriving. At its present headquarters on Locust Street near Thirteenth, the weather-worn Franklin statue and the cornerstone of the original building are exhibited.

Le jeune Benjamin Franklin orgainsa The Library Company of Philadelphia (Cie. d'achats de bibliothèque). On détruisit l'édifice original, mais l'American Philosophical Society fit construir une reproduction sur le même terrain. La compagnie de Franklin, âgée maintenant de plus de 250 ans, prospère toujours. Dans son Centre actuel elle préserve la pierre angulaire de l'édifice original l'inscription de laquelle fut écrite par Franklin. La statue de celui-ci qui se trouvait autrefois au dessus de l'entrée.

Im Jahre 1731 gründete der junge Benjamin Franklin die Library Company of Philadelphia. Das Urgebäude wurde vor einem Jahrhundert abgerissen, aber die American Philosophical Society hat es an derselben Stelle in demselben Stil wiederaufgebaut. Franklins Firma, jetzt beinahe 250 Jahre alt, blüht immer noch. Die jetzige Zentralstelle der Firma bewahrt den Grundstein mit der Inschrift Franklins wie auch eine Statue von ihm, die in dem Urgebäude über der Tür stand.

El joven Benjamin Franklin organizó la Library Congress de Philadelphia en 1731. Su edificio original fue derribado hace un siglo, pero la American Philosophical Society ha puesto una réplica en el mismo sitio. La Company de Franklin todavía prospera, aunque tiene casi más de 250 años. El presente edificio tiene preservada la mocheta que Franklin escribió para el edificio original y una estatua de él encima de la puerta.

This beautiful room in the present building of Benjamin Franklin's Library Company is named in honor of James Logan, the great Philadelphian who came to America with William Penn and in later life was Franklin's friend and adviser. The Library Company is the custodian of the 2000 volume personal library which Logan gave to Philadelphia.

The view of Independence Hall is from a window of Philosophical Hall, headquarters of the prestigious American Philosophical Society founded by Franklin in 1743. Franklin served as president for twenty years. Among his possessions owned by the Society are the folding library chair from his home and a battery of Leyden jars used in his electrical experiments.

Cette belle salle qui se trouve dans l'édifice actuel de la Library Company fondée par Franklin est nommée en honneur de James Logan. La grande bibliothèque que Logan assembla et légua à la ville est toujours préservée dans la Library Company.

Cet aperçu d'Indépendence Hall est pris du bureau central de la prestigieuse American Philosophical Society fondée par Franklin en 1743. La Society possède un nombre des objets de Franklin, y compris le fauteuil de sa bibliothèque et un accumulateur électrique.

Dieses schöne Zimmer, heute ein Teil der Franklin Library Company, wurde James Logan zu Ehren Logan Room benannt. Die grosse Privatbibliothek, die 2000 Bücher umfasst, wurde von Logan zusammengestellt. Diese Büchersammlung, die er der Stadt schenkte, ist noch in der Library Company erhalten.

Dies ist der Blick auf Independence Hall, gesehen von der Zentralstelle der berühmten American Philosophical Society, die Franklin im Jahre 1743 gründete. Diese Gesellschaft ist im Besitz von mehreren Gegenständen, die Franklin gehörten; darunter befinden wir sein Lesestuhl und eine Elektrobatterie.

Esta hermosa cámara en el edificio actual de Franklin's Library Company es nombrado en honor de James Logan. La gran biblioteca personal de unos doscientos tomòs que recogió Logan y diò a la ciudad todavía se mantiene en la Library Company.

La vista de Independence Hall es de la oficina de la prestigiosa "American Philosophical Society" que fundó Franklin en 1743. La sociedad es propietario de muchos bienes de Franklin incluyendo su silla de biblioteca y una batería eléctrica.

At the request of Thomas Bond, physician member of the Philosophical Society, Franklin raised money to establish Pennsylvania Hospital, the first in the colonies. He was one of the original directors, and when the first building was erected in 1755 at Eighth and Spruce Streets, Franklin was the author of the appealing inscription on the cornerstone near the doorway. The original building is used today for offices.

IN THE YEAR OF CHRIST
1755
GEORGE THE SECOND HAPPILY REIGNING;
(FOR HE SOUGHT THE HAPPINESS OF HIS PEOPLE)
PHILADELPHIA FLOURISHING,
(FOR ITS INHABITANTS WERE PUBLICK-SPIRITED)
THIS BUILDING,
BY THE BOUNTY OF THE GOVERNMENT,
AND OF MANY PRIVATE PERSONS
WAS PIOUSLY FOUNDED,
FOR THE RELIEF OF THE SICK AND MISERABLE.
MAY THE GOD OF MERCIES
BLESS THE UNDERTAKING!

Franklin also helped organize a mutual fire insurance company which is still in business—The Philadelphia Contributionship for the Insurance of Houses from Loss by Fire. Its "Hand-in-Hand" firemark with the date of the company's founding, 1752, is a familiar sight on insured properties. The company now occupies a house on Fourth Street near Walnut built in 1836 to serve both as business office and residence of the clerk.

After The Contributionship stopped insuring houses with shade trees because of greater fire hazard, a second insurance company was formed in 1784 by a group of Philadelphians who described themselves: "Proprietors of Houses who have found it convenient and agreeable to them to have trees planted in the Streets before their Houses." Their company, also still thriving, is The Mutual Assurance Company for Insuring Houses from Loss by Fire. Understandably, its firemark is a spreading green tree.

Lemon Hill and Mount Pleasant (below) are country estates of early Philadelphians now owned by the city as part of Fairmount Park.

Lemon Hill was originally the property of Robert Morris, banker, friend of Washington and financier of the Revolution. His mansion was burned during the war. A wealthy merchant later built the present dwelling with the unusual bowed facade which follows the lines of oval-shaped rooms on each of the floors within. He chose the present name of the estate because of the lemon trees Robert Morris had grown in his greenhouse.

Mount Pleasant was built in 1761 on high ground overlooking the Schuylkill. Its occupants included Washington's drill master, Baron von Steuben, and the first Spanish minister to the United States. When he was President and living in Philadelphia, John Adams called Mount Pleasant "the most elegant seat in Pennsylania." The traitor, Benedict Arnold, once purchased the estate as a wedding present for his young Philadelphia bride, but they never lived in it.

Lemon Hill et Mount Pleasant (ci-dessous) sont deux propriétés "de campagne" des premiers Philadelphiens qui appartiennent maintenant à la ville et font partie du Fairmount Park. Lemon Hill fut la propriété de Robert Morris, financier de la Révolution. Mount Pleasant, construit en 1761, fut nommé par John Adams, "le manoir le plus élégant de Pennsylvania."

Lemon Hill und Mount Pleasant (unten) sind zwei von den Landgütern, die den frühen Bewohnern Philadelphias gehörten, und die jetzt als Teil des Fairmount Parks Stadteigentum sind. Lemon Hill war einst das Landgut von Robert Morris, dem Finanzier der Revolution. Mount Pleasant, erbaut 1761, wurde von John Adams als "der eleganteste Landsitz Pennsylvanias" bezeichnet.

Lemon Hill y Mount Pleasant (abajo) son dos haciendas rústicas de los primeros habitantes de Philadelphia que ahora pertenecen a la ciudad y forman parte del Parque Fairmount. Mount Pleasant, edificado en 1761, fue nombrado por John Adams "el sitio más elegante de Pennsylvania".

One of the best of Philadelphia's country estates of colonial days is Woodford, also in Fairmount Park. A small farm house in William Penn's time, it was substantially enlarged and improved by William Coleman, a judge and friend of Franklin, who acquired it in 1756. Once used as a station house by park police, the house has been beautifully restored and furnished by the Naomi Wood estate as "an illustration of household gear during the colonial years." It is included in park house tours conducted by the Philadelphia Museum of Art.

Woodford est une autre propriété coloniale dans le Fairmount Park. Le manoir actuel date de 1756. Il a été meublé par l'agence de Naomi Wood comme "illustration des accoutrements de ménage de la période coloniale."

Woodford ist noch ein kolonialer Landsitz in Fairmount Park. Die heutige Villa stammt aus dem Jahre 1756. Die Naomi Wood Stiftung hat diese Villa "als Beispiel des Haushalts der Kolonialzeit" ausgestattet.

Woodford es otra hacienda rústica y colonial del Parque Fairmount. La mansión de hoy es de 1756. Es amueblada con los bienes de Naomi Wood y "sirve de un ejemplo del estilo colonial de esos días".

Franklin and his wife are buried near the Fifth and Arch Streets corner of Christ Church graveyard. The old brick wall has been opened for a short distance so visitors can see the simple stone which is marked exactly as Franklin directed. Often they leave pennies on the grave of "Poor Richard."

The national memorial to Philadelphia's greatest man is the fine seated statue in Franklin Hall of the Franklin Institute. The Institute's building located on Benjamin Franklin Parkway, was partially financed by a trust which Franklin created for the city.

La tombe de Franklin se trouve dans le cimetière de Christ Church, au coin des rues 5 et Arch. Elle est souvent ornée de pièces de monnaie laissées par les visiteurs en honneur du "Poor Richard." Le monument que la Ville fit dresser pour commémorer Franklin est l'excellente statue dans Franklin Hall de l'Institut Franklin sur l'Avenue Benjamin Franklin.

Franklins Grab steht an dem Begräbnisplatz der Christ Church, Fifth- und Archstrasse. Es wird oft mit dem Kleingeld geschmückt, das von den Besuchern gespendet wird, um "den armen Richard" zu ehren. Das Franklindenkmal der Stadt Philadelphia ist die kunstvolle Statue in der Franklin Hall des Franklin Instituts, das an dem Benjamin Franklin Parkway liegt.

La tumba de Franklin está en el cementerio de Christ Church, calles Fifth y Arch. Está decorada muchas veces de centavos dejados allí por los turistas para honrar "el pobre Richard". El monumento en memoria de Franklin que es de la ciudad es la excelente estatua en Franklin Hall del Franklin Institute que es situado en Benjamin Franklin Parkway.

City of Independence

Le premier Congress Continental se réunit en 1774 dans ce petit hall que le Carpenters' Company (Société des Meunuisiers) venait d'achever. Les députés se réunirent à partir du 5 septembre jusqu'au 26 octobre et ensuite levèrent la séance après avoir arrangé un futur Congress pour 1775, "à moins que la réparation des torts, que nous avons desirée, ne soit effectuée avant ce moment-là." Le Carpenters' Company possède toujours et se réunit dans Carpenters' Hall.

Der erste Kontinentalkongress fand im Jahre 1774 in diesem kleinen Gebäude statt, das zu jener Zeit von der Carpenters Firma erbaut wurde. Die Abgeordneten tagten vom 5. September bis zum 26. Oktober und beendeten ihre Sitzung mit dem Plan, einen zweiten Kongress im Jahre 1775 zusammenzurufen: "es sei denn, die Behebung des Übelstandes, die wir verlangen, wird noch vor dieser Zeit eintreten." Die Firma Carpenter ist immer noch der Besitzer des Gebäudes und gebraucht es heute noch für ihre Sitzungen.

El Primer Congreso Continental se reunió en 1774 en la antecámara pequeña que acababa de haber sido construida por Carpenters' Company. Los diputados trabajaron desde el 5 de Septiembre hasta el 26 de Octubre, y luego suspendieron la sesión después de haber planeado otro congreso para 1775 "a menos de que se obtenga la corrección de los agravios que hemos deseado antes de esa fecha." Carpenters' Company todavía posee y tiene sus reuniones en Carpenters' Hall.

When political tension brought a call for "a congress of Delegates from all the Colonies" in 1774, it was natural that the meeting should be held in Philadelphia.

A new little hall had just been put up near Fourth and Chestnut Streets by a private trade organization, The Carpenters' Company of the City and County of Philadelphia. It was offered to the delegates and was chosen as the meeting place of the First Continental Congress in preference to the Pennsylvania State House two blocks away. The Congress met from September 5 to October 26, 1774 in this first floor room. Upon adjournment, the delegates resolved that another Congress should meet in 1775 "unless the redress of grievances, which we have desired, be obtained before that time."

Carpenters' Hall was located far back on its lot in order to leave room for other buildings which would provide revenue for the Company. The Carpenters' Company, now consisting of about 90 building executives and architects, still owns the historic building, still maintains it and holds its own meetings there.

Within a month after the First Continental Congress adjourned, 28 gentleman members of the Gloucester Fox Hunting Club met in the same building, Carpenters' Hall. They organized themselves into a military unit, The Light Horse of the City of Philadelphia, and offered their services in the approaching conflict with Great Britain. When war came, they served as a reconnaissance force for Washington, were commended by him and eventually became his official escort when he was President.

Since that time, the Troop has served in every time of war and, in colorful uniforms with plumed helmets, has been the escort for United States Presidents on visits to Philadelphia. Officially, the organization is Troop A, First Squadron, 223d Cavalry, Pennsylvania Army Reserve National Guard. Philadelphia calls it The First City Troop.

In November 1974, the Troop celebrated its bicentennial with services at the same colonial church where it first worshipped in 1774—St. Peter's at Fourth and Pine Streets. St. Peter's was built in 1761 and is still maintained by its own congregation to serve an active Episcopal parish.

Vingt-huit membres d'un club de chasse au renard organisèrent une unité militaire à cheval en 1774. Ils servirent sous le Général Washington, devinrent son escorte oficielle pendant sa présidence et depuis ce temps-là l'unité continue à escorter les présidents en visite à Philadelphie. En 1974 cette "First City Troupe" célébra son bicentenaire dans St. Peter's Church, rues 4 et Pine, la même église où ils se réunirent la première fois pour l'exercice du culte en 1774.

Achtundzwanzig Mitglieder eines Fuchs-jagdvereins organisierten 1774 einen berit-tenen Truppenverband. Sie dienten unter Washington, wurden zu seiner offiziellen Eskorte, als er Präsident war, und seit dieser Zeit begleiten sie die Präsidenten während ihrer Besuche in Philadelphia. Im Jahre 1974 feierte der First City Troop sein zwei-hundertjähriges Jubiläum mit einem Gottes-dienst in der St. Peter's Church, also in derselben Kirche, in der die Truppe im Jahre 1774 zum ersten Mal betete.

Veinte y ocho socios de un club para la cacería de zorros organizaron en 1774 un grupo de cabalgadores militares. Le sir-vieron a Washington, se hicieron su escolta oficial cuando era Presidente, y desde en-tonces han acompañado a los Presidentes en sus visitas a Philadelphia. En 1974 La Primera Cuadrilla Ciudadana celebró su bicentenar con servicios en la iglesia Saint Peter, Calles Fourth y Pine, la misma iglesia donde empezó a venerar en 1774.

The Long Room on the second floor of the State House was the scene of many festive occasions. During the meeting of the First Continental Congress the delegates were entertained here by the City of Philadelphia and the Province of Pennsylvania at a magnificent banquet. On that occasion, the first toasts were dutifully raised to members of the British royal family; but—reflecting the temper of the times—the first of many toasts which followed was proposed to "Perpetual Union to the Colonies."

Today's visitors to the 100-foot Long Room hear background music played on a colonial harpsichord.

Au cours des réunions du premier Congress Continental, la ville de Philadelphie et la province de Pennsylvanie reçurent les députés dans un magnifique banquet dans cette salle (Long Room) au premier étage de la Chambre de l'Etat. Les visiteurs d'aujourd 'hui entendent une musique jouée d'un clavecin colonial.

Während des ersten Kontinentalkongresses wurde den Abgeordneten zu Ehren von der Stadt Philadelphia und der Provinz Pennsylvania ein grosses Festessen in diesem Long Room im ersten Stock des State House gehalten. Der heutige Besucher des Saales hört im Hintergrund Cembalomusik aus der Kolonialzeit.

Durante el Primer Congreso Continental, la ciudad de Philadelphia y la Provincia de Pennsylvania les obsequiaron a los diputados con un magnífico banquete en el Long Room del segundo piso de la Casa de Estado. Todos los turistas que visitan esta cámara pueden oír al fondo música tocada por un arpicordio colonial.

The Second Continental Congress also met in Philadelphia, convening on May 10, 1775—this time in the Pennsylvania State House. The fighting at Lexington and Concord had occurred the month before and the "redress of grievances" desired by the First Congress had not been obtained. The delegates provided for a Continental army and designated the Colonel from Virginia, George Washington, as General and Commander-in-Chief. Later in the year, the Navy was established and ships provided for.

The Second Congress met throughout the winter in the large Assembly Room of the State House with John Hancock serving as President. Sentiment for a complete break with Great Britain mounted continuously; and on June 7, 1776, the Virginia delegate Richard Henry Lee offered his resolution "that these United colonies are, and of right ought to be, free and independent States."

Lee's resolution was passed on July 2. While it was under consideration, Thomas Jefferson drafted the Declaration of Independence—intended to justify to the world the passage of the Lee resolution. After considerable amendment, Congress adopted the Declaration late in the afternoon of Thursday, July 4.

The Declaration was not signed that day. Congress merely ordered that the revised text be printed, and then turned to other business. Next day Congress resolved that the Declaration "be proclaimed in each of the United States, and at the Head of the Army." On July 19, it was ordered that the Declaration "be fairly engrossed on parchment . . . and that the same, when engrossed, be signed by every member of Congress."

The formal signing took place on August 2, 1776.

Le deuxième Congress Continental se réunit en mai 1775 et siégea dans la Salle d'assemblée de la Chambre de l'Etat de Pennsylvanie. Il y avait déjà eu du combat à Lexington et Concord dans le Massachusetts et le Congress organisa l'Armée Continentale et nomma George Washington, député de Virginie, commandant en chef.

Le 7 juin 1776, un autre député de Virginie, Richard Henry Lee, suggéra la résolution "que ces colonies Unies sont, et de leur droit devraient être, des Etats libres et indépendants." Le Congress l'adopta le 2 juillet et pour justifier cet acte devant le monde, Thomas Jefferson fut choisi comme rédacteur de la Déclaration d'Indépendance. Après considérables amendements, la Déclaration fut adoptée le 4 juillet mais ce n'est pas avant le 2 août que les membres du Congress signèrent officiellement la Déclaration, "bien rédigée sur parchemin."

Der zweite Kontinentalkongress fand im Mai 1775 statt und tagte in der Versammlungshalle des Pennsylvania State House. Damals wurde bereits bei Lexington und Concord in Massachusetts gekämpft. Der Kongress organisierte die Kontinentalarmee mit George Washington, einem Abgeordneten aus Virginia, als Oberbefehlshaber.

Am. 7. Juni 1776 vertasste Richard Henry Lee, ein anderer Abgeordneter aus Virginia, eine Resolution, die besagte, "dass diese Vereinigten Kolonien frei sind und rechtmässig gesehen, freie und unabhängige Staaten sein müssen." Der Kongress nahm am 2. Juli die Resolution an, und um diese Handlung der Welt gegenüber zu rechtfertigen, wurde Thomas Jefferson beauftragt, den ersten Entwurf der Unabhängigkeitserklärung zu verfassen. Dieses Dokument wurde am 4. Juli mit verschiedenen Änderungen angenommen, aber erst am 2. August 1776 als Urkunde von den Kongressmitgliedern offiziell unterzeichnet.

El Segundo Congreso Continental se reunió en Philadelphia en el mes de Mayo, y celebró la junta en "The Assembly Room" de la Casa de Estado de Pennsylvania. Ya había combates en Lexington y Concord en Massachusetts y por esa causa, el Congreso organizó el Ejército Continental y nombró a George Washington, diputado de Virginia, Generalísimo.

En el 7 de Junio de 1776, otro diputado de Virginia, Richard Henry Lee, ofreció una resolución "estas colonias unidas son y en derecho deben ser estados libres e independientes."

El Congreso la aprobó el 2 de Julio y para justificar esa acción al mundo Thomas Jefferson había sido escogido para escribir la Declaración de Independencia. Después de considerables enmiendas se aprobó la Declaración el 4 de Julio pero la Declaración "primorosamente copiada en pergamino" no fue formalmente firmada por los miembros del Congreso hasta el 2 de Agosto de 1776.

In CONGRESS, July 4, 1776.

The unanimous Declaration of the thirteen united States of America.

and our sacred Honor.

Button Gwinnett
Lyman Hall
Geo Walton.

Wm Hooper
Joseph Hewes,
John Penn

Edward Rutledge.

Thos Heyward Junr.
Thomas Lynch Junr.
Arthur Middleton

John Hancock

Samuel Chase
Wm Paca
Thos Stone
Charles Carroll of Carrollton

George Wythe
Richard Henry Lee
Th Jefferson
Benja Harrison
Thos Nelson jr.
Francis Lightfoot Lee
Carter Braxton

Robt Morris
Benjamin Rush
Benj. Franklin
John Morton
Geo Clymer
Jas Smith
Geo. Taylor
James Wilson
Geo. Ross
Caesar Rodney
Geo Read
Tho M:Kean

Wm Floyd
Phil. Livingston
Frans Lewis
Lewis Morris

Richd Stockton
Jno Witherspoon
Fras Hopkinson
John Hart
Abra Clark

Josiah Bartlett
Wm Whipple
Saml Adams
John Adams
Robt Treat Paine
Elbridge Gerry
Step Hopkins
William Ellery
Roger Sherman
Samel Huntington
Wm Williams
Oliver Wolcott
Matthew Thornton

There was no public celebration of the first Fourth of July. The text of the Declaration was published in Philadelphia newspapers over the weekend, and the entire document was publicly read in the State House yard at noon on Monday, July 8, 1776. Not until then did the great bell in the tower ring out its message of freedom. The bell had no crack at that time. Its inscription: "Proclaim Liberty throughout all the land . . ." had been placed on the bell more than twenty years before.

Il n'y eut pas de célébration publique le 4 juillet 1776. On fit imprimer la Déclaration pendant le week-end et puis on la lut publiquement dans la cour de la Chambre d'Etat le 8 juillet. A ce moment-là le grand bourdon sonna son message de liberté. L'inscription, ". . . proclamerez l'affranchissement de tous les habitants du pays . . ." était sur le bourdon depuis plus de 20 ans.

Keine öffentliche Feier wurde am 4. Juli 1776 veranstaltet. Die Unabhängigkeitserklärung, über das Wochenende gedruckt, wurde am Montag dem 8. Juli bei einer Versammlung im Hofe des State House vorgelesen. Ernst dann läutete die grosse Turmglocke ihre Freiheitskunde. Die Inschrift: "Ihr sollt Freilassung im Lande verkünden", stand schon seit zwanzig Jahren auf dieser Glocke.

No hubo ninguna celebración pública el 4 de julio de 1776. Al terminar el fin de semana se publicó la Declaración y fue leída en una asamblea en el patio de la Casa de Estado el lunes, el 8 de julio. En ese momento tañió desde la torre la gran campana su mensaje de libertad. Hacía más de veinte años que había en la campana la inscripción: "Proclamad la libertad por toda la tierra."

Congress resolved on June 14, 1777, "that the Flag of the United States be thirteen stripes alternate red and white; that the Union be thirteen stars white in a blue field, representing a new constellation." A Philadelphia seamstress, Mrs. Elizabeth Ross, made flags at that time for the government of Pennsylvania. One of the most popular stories of American history is that she cut a star with one snip of her scissors and sewed the first national emblem. A tiny house on Arch Street near Third is the Betsy Ross House and "The Birthplace of Old Glory."

Le Congress adopta le dessin à étoiles et à raies comme le drapeau officiel des Etats-Unis le 14 juin 1777. Une ouvrière-couturière, Mme Elisabeth Ross, faisait des drapeaux pour le gouvernement de Pennsylvanie en ce temps-là. L'histoire qu'elle cousit le premier drapeau rendit célèbre une petite maison dans la rue Arch, désormais connue comme "le Berceau du premier drapeau (Old Glory)."

Der Kongress nahm am 14. Juni 1777 den "Stars and Stripes"—Entwurf für die Fahne der Vereinigten Staaten an. Elizabeth Ross, Schneiderin aus Philadelphia, nähte eine Fahne für die damalige Regierung von Pennsylvania. Die Entstehungsgeschichte der ersten Fahne machte das kleine Haus in der Archstrasse in der Nähe der Thirdstrasse als das Geburtshaus der "Old Glory" berühmt.

El Congreso aprobó el diseño de las estrellas y las rayas como la bandera de los Estados Unidos el 14 de junio de 1777. Una costurera de Philadelphia, la Sra. Elizabeth Ross, hizo en esos días banderas por el gobierno de Pennsylvania. El cuento de cómo cosió ella la primera bandera ha hecho famosa una pequeña casa en la Calle Arch cerca de Third, llamada "el suelo nativo de la anciana gloria."

Six months after the Declaration, the cause of Independence seemed lost. The Continental Army had been defeated in New York and New Jersey and had retreated into Pennsylvania. Congress, fearing capture, had fled Philadelphia. Then General Washington turned the course of the war around by his bold stroke on Christmas night 1776. He recrossed the Delaware River from Pennsylvania to New Jersey, and routed the surprised Hessian mercenaries at Trenton and Princeton.

Two towns, one on each side of the river, are now called Washington Crossing. A state park preserves the historic ground, and every Christmas day men in colonial uniforms re-enact the icy crossing.

The following year, the British General Howe captured Philadelphia from the south after defeating the Continentals at Brandywine Creek. Howe occupied Philadelphia on September 27, 1777; and a week later, Washington attempted another surprise by marching on the city by way of Germantown. This failed, however, and his army went into winter quarters at Valley Forge.

The Battle of Germantown raged around Cliveden, the stone house of Justice Benjamin Chew. It still bears the marks of heavy cannonading.

Avant décembre 1776, la cause de l'indépendance semblait perdue, mais le Général Washington changea le cours de la guerre grâce à une traversée inattendue du fleuve Delaware à Noël. Il mit l'ennemi en déroute et son armée eut le temps de regrouper. Cette traversée historique se refait chaque année le jour de Noël. L'année suivante, après l'occupation par les Anglais, Washington tenta encore une attaque imprévue à Germantown, mais ce fut un échec. La pierre de la maison des Chew, appelée Cliveden, porte encore les traces des cannonades livrées pendant la bataille de Germantown.

Dezember 1776 schien die Unabhängigkeitsbewegung verloren zu sein. General Washington, aber, änderte den Kriegsverlauf am Weihnachtsabend durch eine unerwartete Überfahrt über den Delaware. Er besiegte den Feind und gab damit seinen Truppen die Möglichkeit sich aufs neue zu gruppieren. Diese historische Überfahrt über den Delaware wird jeden Weihnachtstag wiederholt.
Im folgenden Jahr, nachdem Philadelphia von den Engländern besetzt wurde, machte Washington noch einen Überraschungsangriff auf Germantown, aber diese Taktik misslang. Das Steinblockhaus der Familie Chew, Cliveden, zeigt heute noch die Spuren der Kanonade des Kampfes um Germantown.

En diciembre, 1776, pareció perdida la causa, pero el General Washington cambió el rumbo de la guerra cuando atrevesó sin aviso el río Delaware la noche de Navidad. El año próximo, después de que Philadelphia había sido ocupada por los ingleses, intentó otro ataque de improviso en Germantown, pero fracasó el esfuerzo. La casa de piedra le los Chew, llamada Cliveden, todavía muestra marcas causadas por los cañonazos durante la Batalla de Germantown.

The winter of 1777-78 was just beginning when Washington's army arrived at Valley Forge, about 20 miles northwest of Philadelphia. At first his soldiers endured unbelievable hardships while the camp was being organized and huts built for living quarters. Only General Washington's character and determination held the army together until supplies of food and clothing could be obtained.

Although the British in Philadelphia greatly outnumbered the troops with Washington, no serious effort was made to attack. On the contrary, the British found many friends and genial Tory hosts in Philadelphia and eventually settled into a busy winter round of dinners, dances and theatre parties.

Woodford Mansion, owned at that time by David Franks, agent of the Crown, was the scene of frequent entertainment. One of Frank's daughters married a British officer and General Howe was said to have been a regular visitor.

L'hiver commençait à peine quand l'armée de Washington établissait un camp à Valley Forge, à 20 miles de Philadelphie. Les troupes en lambeaux et affamées supportèrent d'incroyables épreuves avant d'obtenir des vivres et de terminer l'organisation de leur camp. Entretemps, les Anglais, officiers et soldats, passèrent un hiver confortable dans la ville, reçus régulièrement dans les maisons partisanes des Tory et souvent dans le manoir à Woodford.

Der Winter hatte gerade begonnen, als Washingtons Armee ins Winterlager bei Valley Forge, 20 Meilen von Philadelphia entfernt, einzog. Die zerlumpten und hungrigen Soldaten litten unglaubhafte Not, ehe sie Proviant bekamen und das Lager aufschlugen. Inzwischen verbrachten die englischen Offiziere und Soldaten die Zeit angenehm in der Stadt, wo sie in den Häusern von Toryfreunden und oft im Woodford Mansion bewirtet wurden.

Empezando el invierno, el ejército de Washington acampó en Valley Forge, unas 20 millas de Philadelphia. Los trapajosos y hambrientes tropeles sufrían privaciones increíbles antes de que recibieron provisiones y organizaron el campamento. Mientras tanto, los oficiales ingleses y los suyos pasaban una temporada cómoda en la ciudad, siempre obsequiados en las casas de los partidarios de los conservadores, y a menudo en la mansión Woodford.

The rolling countryside of Valley Forge is beautiful in mild weather; and by the time the spring of 1778 arrived, the condition of Washington's army had greatly improved. The men were better housed, better fed and better clothed. Then, the spirits of all were lifted by news of the French Alliance which Benjamin Franklin had negotiated in Paris. The Commander ordered an entire day of Thanksgiving and celebration at Valley Forge—there were prayer services, enthusiastic marches on the parade ground and the sound of musket fire echoing through the hills at night.

In Philadelphia, news of French aid for the cause of Independence led General Howe at once to begin planning evacuation of the city. He remembered the year before.

When the British first took Philadelphia, their supply situation had been desperate. Washington's army cut off land routes, and British naval units were unable to penetrate the defenses of the Delaware River. It took nearly a week of intense bombardment of tiny Fort Mifflin, just below Philadelphia, before the river was opened. The heroics of Continental soldiers during that siege are regularly re-enacted at Fort Mifflin today.

Quand de printemps vint à Valley Forge, la condition de l'armée de Washington s'améliora. Les nouvelles de l'alliance avec la France arrivèrent et l'esprit de corps monta. A Philadelphie, les Anglais inaugura immédiatement des projets pour s'échapper.

Als es Frühling in Valley Forge wurde, verbesserte sich die Lage von Washingtons Armee. Die Nachricht über das Bündnis mit Frankreich erreichte sie und stärkte den Mut der Soldaten. In Philadelphia machten die Engländer Pläne die Stadt unverzüglich zu räumen.

Cuando llegó la primavera en Valley Forge, la situación del ejército de Washington se mejoró. Llegaron las noticias de una alianza con Francia y se elevaron los espíritus. En Philadelphia, los ingleses inmediatamente empezaron a hacer planes para evacuar la ciudad.

The British withdrew from Philadelphia in June 1778. Congress promptly returned, and on July 9, eight states signed the new Articles of Confederation. Most of the war thereafter was fought in the South, and it came to an end at Yorktown in 1781. In Washington Square in Philadelphia, the tomb of an unknown soldier of the Continental Army is a memorial to all who gave their lives for Independence.

After the fighting ended, a number of Quakers who had supported the Revolutionary cause and had been disowned by their own meetings for doing so, established the Free Quaker Meeting and built this attractive little meeting house at Fifth and Arch Streets. The Meeting is no longer active and the building is now part of Independence Mall.

The date stone on the north wall of the Free Quaker Meeting House testifies to the uncertainty of the times about government under the Articles of Confederation. Beginning with 1776, the author of the inscription calculated 1783 to be the eighth year "of the Empire."

La Guerre d'Indépendance se termina à Yorktown en 1781. La tombe d'un soldat continental inconnu au Square Washington à Philadelphie est un monument commémoratif à tous ceux qui sont morts pour la nation naissante.

Le combat terminé, les Quakers de Philadelphie à qui on avait défendu l'entrée dans leurs propres services ou "Meetings" pour avoir sympathisé avec les Anglais, organisèrent le Free Quaker Meeting et firent construire une Meeting House dans les rues 5 et Race. Cette House n'est plus en état de servir.

Der Unabhängigkeitskrieg endete 1781 bei Yorktown. Das Grab eines Unbekannten Soldaten der Kontinentalen Armee, das auf dem Washington Square in Philadelphia steht, ist ein Denkmal zu Ehren aller, die ihr Leben für die junge Nation hingaben.

Als der Krieg zu Ende war, gründeten die Quäker von Philadelphia, die aus dem Quäkerbund wegen Kriegsbeteiligung ausgeschlossen wurden, das Free Quaker Meeting und errichteten ein Meeting House an der Ecke von Fifth- und Archstrasse. Es hat heute keine aktiven Mitglieder.

La Guerra de Independencia finalizó en Yorktown en 1781. La tumba del soldado desconocido de esta guerra en la Plaza de Washington, Philadelphia, es en memoria a todos los que murieron por la joven nación.

Cuando terminó la lucha, los cuáqueros de Philadelphia cuyos servicios religiosos habían sido prohibidos por haber soportado la guerra, organizaron la Asamblea de Cuáqueros Libres y construyeron una Casa de Asamblea en las Calles Fifth y Arch. Ya no es activa esta casa.

Delegates from the several states (no longer colonies) came back to Philadelphia on May 25, 1787 for a Convention called to revise the inadequate Articles of Confederation. They ended by drawing up a whole new frame of government—the Constitution of the United States.

The Convention gathered in the Assembly Room where the Declaration of Independence had been adopted eleven years before, and George Washington was chosen to preside. All through a hot, humid summer he guided the long and difficult debates, trying to find compromises which would unite the northern states and the southern states, the large states and the small ones.

The task was completed and the Constitution approved by the Convention on September 17, 1787. Pennsylvania's aged delegate Benjamin Franklin called attention to the carving on the back of Washington's chair. "Now at length," said he, "I have the happiness to know that it is a rising and not a setting sun."

We the People of the United ...

insure domestic Tranquility, provide for the common defence, promote the ... and our Posterity, do ordain and establish this Constitution for the United ...

Article. I.

Section. 1. All legislative Powers herein granted shall be vested in a Cong... of Representatives.

Section. 2. The House of Representatives shall be composed of Members cho... in each State shall have the Qualifications requisite for Electors of the most numerous B... No Person shall be a Representative who shall not have attained to the A... and who shall not, when elected, be an Inhabitant of that State in which he shall be c... Representatives and direct Taxes shall be apportioned among the several State...

Les députés des états (non plus des colonies) revinrent à Philadelphie en 1787 pour la Convention qui dressa la Constitution des Etats-Unis. Elle fut ratifiée le 17 septembre 1787. Le Député Benjamin Franklin exprima sa joie de savoir enfin que la sculpture au dossier du fauteuil du président représentait un lever et non pas un coucher de soleil.

Abgeordnete von den Staaten (nicht mehr Kolonien) kamen 1787 nach Philadelphia zurück, um im Konvent die Verfassung der Vereinigten Staaten auszuarbeiten. Den 17. September 1787 wurde die Bundesverfassung approbiert. Der Abgeordnete Benjamin Franklin sagte, es bereite ihm eine grosse Freude endlich zu erfahren, dass der Holzschnitt an der Rücklehne des Stuhles des Vorsitzenden eine aufgehende und keine untergehende Sonne darstelle.

Los diputados de los Estados (ya no colonias) volvieron a Philadelphia en 1787 para la Convención que redactó la Constitución de los Estados Unidos. La aprobación final fue hecha en el 17 de Septiembre de 1787. El diputado Benjamin Franklin dijo que se alegró de saber que por fin el respaldo de la silla del oficial que preside la asamblea representa un sol naciente y no un sol poniente.

George Washington's Capital City

George Washington was inaugurated President, and the first Congress met in 1790 in New York City. Within a few months, it was decided that a new "Federal City" would be established on the Potomac between Maryland and Virginia, and that, while it was being built, Philadelphia would be the capital of the United States.

Fine quarters were available here. The City of Philadelphia had just completed two new buildings which extended the State House complex to the entire Chestnut Street block from Fifth to Sixth Streets as it is today. From 1790 until 1800, the Supreme Court of the United States sat in the little building on the corner of Fifth Street which had been put up as a City Hall. The somewhat larger building at Sixth Street was turned over to Congress and has been known ever since as Congress Hall. The United States Senate sat in the ornate chamber on the second floor. Since three states were added to the original thirteen while the capital was here, the number of Senators' desks was increased to 32.

The Powel House, built in 1765 on Third Street near Spruce, was one of the finest houses in colonial Philadelphia. It was the home of Samuel Powel, a merchant who was also Mayor of the city in 1776. During the occupation of the city, it was used by the British High Commissioner. Later, when Philadelphia was the capital, George and Martha Washington were frequently guests here, and the Powels visited at Mount Vernon.

A much more modest house nearby at Fourth and Walnut was the home of the widow, Dolley Payne Todd. While Congress was in session in Philadelphia, one of the Virginia representatives, James Madison, asked to meet her. They were married in 1794. When Madison became President of the United States fifteen years later, Dolley Madison acquired fame as a White House hostess.

La maison Powel, dans la 3ème rue près de la rue Spruce, était l'une des plus élégantes de Philadelphie. Pendant sa présidence Washington y fut souvent invité. Dans une maison plus modeste dans les rues 4 et Walnut, demeurait une veuve, Dolley Payne Todd. A l'époque où le Congress se réunissait tout près elle se maria avec l'un des délégués de Virginie, James Madison. Après l'élection de son mari à la présidence des Etats-Unis, Dolley Madison devint célèbre en qualité d'hôtess de la Maison Blanche.

Das Powel House in der Thirdstrasse in der Nähe der Sprucestrasse war eines der elegantesten Häuser des frühen Philadelphia. Als Washington Präsident war, weitte er hier oft zu Besuch. In einem bescheidenerem Haus an der Ecke der Fourth- und Walnutstrasse, lebte eine Witwe namens Dolley Payne Todd. Da der Kongress in der Nähe tagte, lernte sie den Abgeordneten aus Virginia James Madison kennen, den sie heiratete. Als er zum Präsidenten der Vereinigten Staaten gewählt wurde, wurde Dolley Madison als Gastgeberin des Weissen Hauses berühmt.

La Casa Powell, en la Calle Third cerca de Spruce, fue una de las más elegantes casas de la joven Philadelphia. Cuando Washington fue Presidente, era frecuentemente un huésped en esa casa. En una casa más modesta en las Calles Fourth y Walnut, vivía una viuda, Dolly Payne Todd. Durante las cercanas reuniones del Congreso, ella y uno de los representantes de Virginia, James Madison, se casaron. Cuando él llegó a ser Presidente de los Estados Unidos, Dolly Madison se hizo una famosa anfitriona de la Casa Blanca.

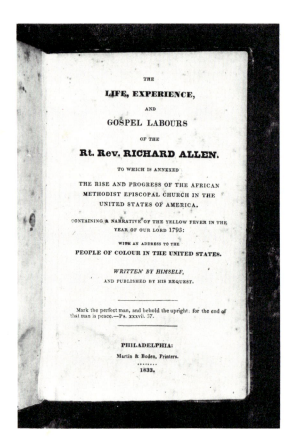

THE

LIFE, EXPERIENCE,

AND

GOSPEL LABOURS

OF THE

Rt. Rev. RICHARD ALLEN.

TO WHICH IS ANNEXED

THE RISE AND PROGRESS OF THE AFRICAN
METHODIST EPISCOPAL CHURCH IN THE
UNITED STATES OF AMERICA.

CONTAINING A NARRATIVE OF THE YELLOW FEVER IN THE
YEAR OF OUR LORD 1793:

WITH AN ADDRESS TO THE

PEOPLE OF COLOUR IN THE UNITED STATES.

WRITTEN BY HIMSELF,
AND PUBLISHED BY HIS REQUEST.

Mark the perfect man, and behold the upright: for the end of
that man is peace.—Ps. xxxvii. 37.

PHILADELPHIA:
Martin & Boden, Printers.
1833.

MOTHER BETHEL
AFRICAN METHODIST EPISCOPAL CHURCH
FOUNDED ON THIS SITE 1787
BY
RICHARD ALLEN
(A FORMER SLAVE)

THIS GROUND, PURCHASED BY RICHARD ALLEN
FOR A CHURCH, IS THE OLDEST PARCEL OF REAL
ESTATE OWNED CONTINUOUSLY BY NEGROES
IN THE UNITED STATES. THIS CONGREGATION
IS THE WORLD'S OLDEST AFRICAN METHODIST
EPISCOPAL CHURCH CONGREGATION.

• • •

THE FIRST CHURCH (1787) WAS AN ABANDONED
BLACKSMITH SHOP, HAULED TO THIS PLACE BY
THE TEAMS OF RICHARD ALLEN WHO WAS
ELECTED A BISHOP IN 1816.

"WE ALL WENT OUT OF THE CHURCH (OLD ST. GEORGE'S
METHODIST CHURCH) IN A BODY" AND "THEY WERE NO
MORE PLAGUED WITH US IN THEIR CHURCH."
RICHARD ALLEN

• • •

MAY OUR GOD CONTINUE TO BLESS MOTHER BETHEL AND ALL
HER CHILDREN, NOW SCATTERED THROUGHOUT THE WORLD,
BRINGING FAITH AND HOPE TO MILLIONS OF WEARY SOULS.

RING THE BELLS OF FREEDOM
THROUGHOUT THE WORLD
•
"RISE, SHINE, GIVE GOD THE GLORY
FOR THE YEAR OF JUBILEE."
OCTOBER 1961

Richard Allen, born a slave in Philadelphia in 1760, acquired an education, bought his freedom at age 17 and became both businessman and clergyman. He hauled salt for the Continental army and he belonged to historic St. George's Methodist Church where he regularly preached at the early morning service.

In 1787, when black worshippers at St. George's were directed to a segregated balcony, Allen and another minister, Absalom Jones, led a walkout from the church. They formed the Free African Society and conducted religious services in a rented storehouse. Absalom Jones united with the Church of England and founded St. Thomas African Protestant Episcopal Church. Its original building was near Fifth and Walnut Streets but St. Thomas is now located in West Philadelphia.

Richard Allen remained a Methodist. He bought an old frame shack which had been a blacksmith shop, hauled it to the lot he owned on Sixth Street near Lombard and made it the first home of Mother Bethel Church which occupies the same site.

Allen obtained a state charter for the independent church in 1796. Twenty years later, the first conference of the African Methodist Episcopal Church was held at Mother Bethel, and Richard Allen became the first bishop. He died in 1831, and is interred in the present church building. Congress has designated Mother Bethel as a national historical landmark.

Richard Allen, ancien esclave, homme d'affaires et pasteur, acheta un terrain en 1787 y transporta une forge abandonnée, et y établit Mother Bethel Church, rues 6 et Lombard. Il devint le premier évêque de l'Eglise African Methodist Episcopal. Son église occupe toujours le même terrain. La tombe de Richard Allen se trouve dans l'église-même. Elle a été nommée un monument national historique.

Richard Allen, ehemaliger Sklave, Geschäftsmann, und Geistlicher schaffte sich im Jahre 1787 ein Grundstück an, brachte eine verlassene Schmiede an die Stelle und gründete Mother Bethel Church an der Sixthstrasse in der Nähe der Lombardstrasse. Er wurde zum ersten Bischof der African Methodist Episcopal Church. Seine Kirche steht immer noch auf demselben Platz. Richard Allens Grab ist in diesem Gebäude, das jetzt eine national-historische Erinnerungsstätte ist.

Richard Allen, antes un esclavo, hombre de negocios y clérigo, compró terreno en 1787, lo convirtió a una herrería, y estableció la iglesia Mother Bethel en la Calle 6th cerca de Lombard. El se hizo el primer obispos de la iglesia episcopal llamada African Methodist. Su iglesia todavía es situada en el mismo sitio. La tumba de Richard Allen está en el edificio, ha sido nombrado una marca nacional e historica.

When a terrible plague of yellow fever swept Philadelphia in 1793, many government officials including President Washington fled the city. For a brief period that fall and again in 1794, a comfortable home at 5442 Germantown Avenue served as a temporary White House. With the Washingtons in residence, cabinet meetings were held here and the business of government was conducted in these rooms. Known as the Deshler-Morris House for two of its owners, the property is now in the care of Independence National Historical Park.

Early Philadelphia companies often held board meetings in the late afternoon and afterwards served dinner in lieu of paying fees to the directors. Such a dinner was in progress at the Mutual Assurance Company in December 1799 when news arrived of the death of George Washington at Mount Vernon. It was terminated at once in tribute to the great man so many directors had known personally.

The company's directors now meet monthly at its headquarters in historic Shippen-Wistar House at Fourth and Locust Streets and dine afterward in this beautiful old room. At the end of the meal, the dinner-jacketed directors rise, face the portrait on the east wall and adjourn with a toast "to the memory of General Washington."

Parmi les souvenirs de George Washington on peut conter la maison Deshler-Morris à Germantown qui servit de Maison Blanche provisoire en 1793, et aussi les dîners des directeurs de la Mutual Assurance Company qui se terminent toujours avec le toast traditionnel porté au souvenir du premier président.

Unter den verschiedenen Gebäuden, die die Erinnerung an George Washington wachhalten, befindet sich das Deshler-Morris House in Germantown, das 1793 als provisorisches Weisses Haus diente. Ebenso erinnern die Dinner der Direktoren der Mutual Assurance Company mit ihrem traditionellen Toast an den ersten Präsidenten, an George Washington.

Unos recuerdos de George Washington en Philadelphia incluyen la casa Deshler/Morris en Germantown que servía de una provisional Casa Blanca en 1793, y también de un lugar para las cenas de los directores de la Compañia Mutual Assurance, que todavía terminan con el brindis tradicional a la memoria del primer Presidente.

When the United States government moved to Washington, D.C., Congress presented Ceracchi's bust of Liberty to the Library Company of Philadelphia in appreciation for its service for over a quarter of a century. The Franklin-founded company had been quite literally the unofficial Library of Congress. It had been located on the second floor of Carpenters' Hall in 1774 while the First Continental Congress was meeting downstairs. Later, it served the Second Continental Congress as well; and after formation of the union, the Library Company was located in its own building just across Fifth Street from where Congress sat.

The first "Statue of Liberty" now occupies a place of honor in the present home of the Library Company at 1314 Locust Street. There, too, the very books, newspapers and handbills that were read by the first leaders of the United States are still available in the stacks.

In Carpenters' Hall, the second floor now houses the books of the Carpenters' Company itself. Some of the volumes date back to the Company's founding in 1724.

Au moment où le premier Congress Continental se réunissait dans le Carpenters' Hall, la Library Company fondée par Franklin se trouvait au premier étage de cet édifice. Des livres et des journaux que l'on lisait alors sont encore dans la bibliothèque actuelle de la Company. Au premier étage du Carpenters' Hall on trouve aujourd'hui les livres de l'ancienne Carpenters' Company. Quelques-uns portent la date de sa fondation, 1724.

Als der erste Kontinentalkongress in der Carpenters' Hall tagte, befand sich die von Franklin gegründete Library Company im ersten Stock des Gebäudes. Bücher und Zeitungen aus damaliger Zeit befinden sich heute noch auf den Bücherregalen der Zentralstelle der Firma. Im ersten Stock der Carpenters' Hall findet man die Bücher der Firma Carpenters, die auf das Gründungsjahr 1724 zurückgehen.

Mientras que El Primer Congreso Continental se runió en Carpenters' Hall, the Library Company, que Franklin fundó, estaba situada en el segundo piso de ese edificio. Unos libros y periódicos utilizados en esos días todavía están en los estantes del edificio actual de the Company. El segundo piso de Carpenters' Hall alberga los libros de Carpenters' Company, algunos publicados en 1724, el año de su fundación.

A central Bank of the United States ("First Bank") was organized in 1791 under Alexander Hamilton, Washington's Secretary of the Treasury. It came to an end in 1811 when Congress refused to renew its charter, but the banking house remains on Third Street near Chestnut. Philadelphia's Stephen Girard bought the building and operated his own private bank there until his death.

Pendant la présidence de Washington, on établit une banque centrale des Etats-Unis. En 1811 elle cessa d'exister, mais sa maison dans la 3ème rue près de la rue Chestnut continue à être de grand intérêt dans l'Independence National Historical Park.

Während Washingtons Amtszeit wurde eine zentrale Bank der Vereinigten Staaten gegründet. Seit 1811 existiert sie nicht mehr, aber das Bankgebäude in der Thirdstrasse in der Nähe der Chestnutstrasse ist heute noch eine der Sehenswürdigkeiten des Independence National Historical Park.

Durante la presidencia de Washington se estableció un banco central de los Estados Unidos. Aunque se acabó en 1811, su casa de banco en la Calle Third cerca de Chestnut se queda una de las atracciones en Independence National Historical Park.

Another of old Philadelphia's architectural gems is The Merchants' Exchange at Third and Walnut Streets, built in 1832. It became the first permanent home of the Philadelphia Stock Exchange. The Stock Exchange was founded in 1790, and its business was transacted originally in the city's coffee houses. The Merchants' Exchange building is now used for administrative offices of the National Park Service.

Le Merchants' Exchange, rues 3 et Walnut, construit en 1832, fut la première maison permanente de la Bourse de Philadelphie. L'édifice est actuellement occupé par les bureaux administratifs du Service National des Parcs.

Die Kaufmannsbörse (Merchant's Exchange), 3rd & Walnut, gebaut in 1832, war das erste dauernde heim der Philadelphia Aktien-Börse. Gegründet in 1790, all verhandlung war abgemacht in örtlich kaffeehäuser. Die Kaufmannsbörse wird jetzt für National Park verwaltung verwendet.

Un otro preciosidad arquitectural de Filadelfia viejo esta La Plaza de Contratacion de Mercaderes a las calles Tercero y Walnut, construido en 1832. La llegó la primera casa permanente de La Bolsa Filadelfia. La Bolsa fundarse en 1790, y comercio originalmente negociada en los cafés de la ciudad. El edificio de La Plaza de Contratacion de Mercaderes, ahora, esta usada por las oficinas administrativa del Servicio Parque Nacional.

Talented artists congregated in Philadelphia to earn their living doing portraits of leaders of the Revolution and of the Federal Government. One, Charles Willson Peale, began painting soldiers at Valley Forge and eventually filled a museum which he operated in the Long Room of Independence Hall for a quarter of a century. Peale was one of the founders of the Pennsylvania Academy of Fine Arts in 1805.

Some eighty of the Peale portraits and about one hundred others are now collected in a captivating Portrait Gallery maintained at Independence National Historical Park. Centerpiece of the exhibit is the historic wooden statue of George Washington originally carved for Independence Hall by William Rush.

The beautiful building which has become the permanent home of the Park's collection was built in 1819 for the Bank of the United States ("Second Bank") which Congress created in 1816. Located on Chestnut Street between Fourth and Fifth, this served as the Philadelphia Custom House for nearly a century after the Bank was terminated.

Dans l'Independence National Historical Park on a créé un musée de portraits des chefs de la guerre révolutionnaire et du jeune gouvernement fédéral. Peints par des artistes de l'époque, ces portraits sont en exposition dans un bel édifice de la rue Chestnut entre les rues 4 et 5, construit originalement pour la Banque des Etats-Unis en 1819.

Eine Gemäldegalerie des Befreiungskrieges mit einer Porträtsammlung der führenden Bundesbeamten, von zeitgenössischen Künstlern gemalt, wurde von den zuständigen Behörden des Independence National Historical Parks zusammengestellt. Sie befindet sich in einer Dauerausstellung in dem schönen Gebäude in der Chestnutstrasse zwischen der Fourth- und Fifthstrasse, das ursprünglich 1819 als Bank der Vereinigten Staaten gebaut wurde.

Independence National Historical Park ha creado una permanente galería de retratos de la guerra de la Revolución y de los primeros líderes del gobierno federal pintados por los artistas de la época. Estos están exhibidos en el bello edificio en la Calle Chestnut entre Fourth y Fifth, originalmente edificado en 1819 por el Banco de los Estados Unidos.

Philadelphia Today

Benjamin Franklin Parkway, a broad, tree-lined boulevard, sweeps directly from center city to the palatial Philadelphia Museum of Art on a hilltop at the entrance to Fairmount Park. Midway, the Parkway curves around a circular fountain at Logan Square. Near City Hall, it meets John F. Kennedy Plaza and the Tourist Information Center of the Philadelphia Convention and Visitors' Bureau.

L'Avenue Benjamin Franklin s'étend du centre de la ville jusqu'au Musée d'art et au Parc Fairmount. Près de l'Hôtel de Ville l'Avenue aboutit à la Place John F. Kennedy où se trouve le Centre des Renseignements touristiques de la Ville.

Der Benjamin Franklin Parkway erstreckt sich vom Stadtzentrum bis an das Philadelphia Kunstmuseum und den Fairmount Park. In der Nähe des Rathauses mündet der Parkway beim städtischen Verkehrsamt in den John F. Kennedy Platz.

Benjamin Franklin Parkway pasa majestuosamente en una línea recta desde el centro de la ciudad hasta el Museo de Arte de Philadelphia y el Parque Fairmount. Cerca del Ayuntamiento se junta con la Plaza John F. Kennedy y el Centro de Información Turística de la ciudad.

Philadelphia's monumental City Hall stands at the intersection of Broad Street and Market Street—the two main thoroughfares of Penn's original plan. It occupies a full city block, a massive structure of granite and marble, richly ornamented with architectural devices and more than 300 statues and carvings. The foundation walls which carry the stone building are over twenty feet thick. Workmen required more than twenty years to complete City Hall, including the tower topped by the founder's statue.

The unique stone stairways in City Hall include one in the south entrance which leaps upward two floors at a time. The ornate Mayor's Reception Room is the locale for ceremonies which range from press conferences to awards for police heroism. Near the top of City Hall tower is an observation platform for sightseers.

L'Hôtel de Ville de Philadelphie est un monument en pierre au carrefour des deux rues principales disposées sur le plan original de Penn. Il est richement orné de 300 statues et sculptures. Toutes sortes de cérémonies municipales ont lieu dans la Salle de Reception du Maire. Près du haut de la tour de l'Hôtel de Ville se trouve une plate-forme d'observation pour visiteurs.

Das Rathaus von Philadelphia ist ein monumentaler Steinbau, der an der Kreuzung der zwei Hauptstrassen liegt, wie schon in Penns ursprünglichem Plan vermerkt wurde. Es ist durch eine übertrieben schwere Pracht gekennzeichnet; aus etwa 300 Statuen und Schnitzwerken. Das Empfangszimmer des Bürgermeisters wird für verschiedene städtische Veranstaltungen benutzt. Auf der Spitze des Rathausturmes befindet sich eine Plattform, die dem Besucher eine Aussicht auf die Stadt bietet.

El ayuntamiento de Philadelphia es una monumental estructura de piedra situada en la intersección de las dos calles principales indicadas en el plan original de Penn. Es ricamente decorado de trescientas estatuas y esculturas. La Cámara de recibimiento del Alcalde es el lugar para ceremonias municipales de muchas clases. Cerca de la cumbre de la torre del Ayuntamiento hay un observatorio por los visitantes.

Around City Hall, directly below the Founder's statue, Philadelphia presents an outstanding demonstration of progressive mid-city urban renewal. Within a relatively few years, the entire heart of the city has taken on a new appearance. Penn Center and City Hall West Plaza have replaced the old Pennsylvania Railroad passenger station; the towers of Centre Square rise above the intricate dome of a lofty galleria; and in front of The Fidelity Mutual Life Building at Three Girard Plaza, the 28 foot Triune symbolizes in bronze the unity of people, industry and government in Penn's city.

En relativement peu de temps, le coeur de Philadelphie a été transformé par la modernisation urbaine. Les tours jumelles de Centre Square dominent une galerie à dôme vitré, et l'esprit de la ville se symbolise dans la Triade en bronze, haute de 26 pieds, qui est devant le Fidelity Mutual Life Building.

In verhältnismässig wenigen Jahren ist das Herz Philadelphias durch die moderne Stadtplanung verwandelt worden. Die Zwillingstürme am Centre Square erheben sich über einer mit Glas überdachten Galerie. Der Geist der Stadt wird symbolisiert durch eine 26 Fuss hohe Bronzestatue vor dem Fidelity Mutual Life Building.

Dentro de unos pocos años, el centro de Philadelphia ha estado transformado por una urbanización moderna. Las dobles torres de Centre Square surgen encima de una galería con una cúpula de vidrio, y el espíritu de la ciudad es simbolizado por el Trino de bronce que mide veinte y seis pies y que está situado enfrente del edificio Fidelity Mutual Life.

Philadelphia offers many reminders of Paris, among them these twin buildings at Logan Square, 19th Street and the Parkway, which are modeled after the Place de la Concorde. The one at the left is the Free Library of Philadelphia; the other houses the Municipal Court.

Ces édifices jumeaux à Logan Square, 19ème rue et Avenue B. Franklin, font souvenir de la Place de la Concorde à Paris. Celui à gauche est la Bibliothèque principale de Philadelphie (Free Library); l'autre est la Cour de Justice municipale.

Die Zwillingsgebäude am Logan Square, an der Kreuzung der Nineteenthstrasse und des Parkway, erinnern den Besucher an den Place de la Concorde in Paris. Das Gebäude links ist die Freie Bibliothek der Stadt Philadelphia; das andere ist das städtische Gerichtshaus.

Estos semejantes edificios en Logan Square, Calle 19 y el Parkway, son recuerdos de la Place de la Concorde en Paris. El de la izquierda es the "Free Library" de Philadelphia; el otro es la casa del "Municipal Court."

Stephen Girard, French merchant and banker, settled in Philadelphia in 1776. When he died in 1831, a widower without children, he left his large estate to the City to establish a residential school for young orphan boys. Called Girard College, it is located in North Philadelphia on what was one of his farms. Girard is interred here in Founder's Hall and the School is still maintained by his estate.

Stephen Girard, négociant et banquier français qui vécut à Philadelphie, 1776-1831, légua toute sa fortune à la Ville pour fonder Girard College, une école pour garçons orphelins. L'école est située sur une ancienne propriété qui avait été l'une des fermes de Girard. Celui-ci est enterré à Philadelphie dans le Founder's Hall.

Stephen Girard, ein französischer Kaufman und Bankier, der von 1776 bis 1831 in Philadelphia lebte, hinterliess sein grosses Vermögen der Stadt, um Girard College, eine Waisenschule für Knaben, zu gründen. Die Schule befindet sich dort, wo in der Vergangenheit seine Farm lag. Girard wurde in der Founder's Hall begraben.

Stephen Girard, comerciante y banquero francés quien vivió en Philadelphia desde 1776 hasta 1831, dejó su gran hacienda a la ciudad para establecer "Girard College," una escuela para los huérfanos. Está situado en lo que fue uno de sus estancias, y Girard está enterrado aquí en Founders' Hall.

The Philadelphia Museum of Art is a treasure house of masterpieces: a magnificent Greco-Roman temple crowning the hill and overlooking the downtown skyline, the Schuylkill and Fairmount Park.

This city-owned Museum contains ten acres of space, a hundred galleries and rooms, and more than 100,000 works of art. Along with outstanding painting and sculpture, it houses exhibits of tapestries, furniture, furnishings and fashions. Period rooms and architectural units have been assembled from many parts of the world, one of the most handsome being the Eighteenth-century drawing room from Lansdowne House, a fine townhouse in London's Berkeley Square.

Le Musée d'art de Philadelphie est un trésor de chefs-d'oeuvre de tous les siècles. En plus de ses peintures et sculptures exceptionnelles il contient des expositions de tapisseries, de meubles, et de mode.

Das Kunstmuseum von Philadelphia beherbergt die Meisterwerke vieler Jahrhunderte. Es enthält hervorragende Gemälde und Skulpturen, Tapeten, Möbel, und Trachten aus vergangenen Zeiten.

El Museo de Arte de Philadelphia es un tesoro de obras maestras de todos los siglos. Además de las importantes obras de pintura y de escultura, alberga unas exhibiciones de tapices, muebles, mobilarios y modas.

The Philadelphia Orchestra is admired and honored all over the world, but nowhere more than at home. In addition to its foreign travels and out-of-town engagements, the Orchestra plays about a hundred concerts each year to capacity audiences in its own beautiful hall, the Academy of Music at Broad and Locust Streets. The Academy was built in 1853, and is now the property of The Philadelphia Orchestra Association. The Orchestra was established in 1900.

L'Orchestre de Philadelphie est admiré et estimé partout dans le monde, mais en aucun lieu autant que dans sa ville. Chaque année il présente à peu près cent concerts dans sa propre belle salle, toujours complète, qui s'appelle l'Academy of Music.

Das Philadelphia Orchester hat Weltruf und ist auch zu Hause sehr beliebt. Jedes Jahr werden über einhundert gutbesuchte Konzerte in der schönen Halle der Academy of Music veranstaltet.

La Orchesta de Philadelphia es admirada y honrada por todas partes del mundo, pero especialmente en su pueblo natal. Cada año da más de cien conciertos a un público completamente lleno, en un bello teatro que se llama la Academia de Música.

Subscription concerts are given at home by the Philadelphia Orchestra on Tuesday, Thursday, Friday and Saturday nights and on Friday afternoons. Philadelphians identify themselves to friends by the concert attended. From season to season they send in ticket orders early, hoping to acquire seniority in choice of seats. In summer, the Orchestra presents a five-week series of outdoor concerts at Robin Hood Dell in Fairmount Park. No admission is charged, and often the audience is as large as 30,000.

Des concerts d'abonnement sont présentés par l'orchestre de Philadelphie dans l'Academy les mardi, jeudi, et samedi soirs et aussi les vendredi après-midi. En été cinq semaines de concerts en plein air sont présentés à Robin Hood Dell dans le Fairmount Park où assistent jusqu'à 30.000 personnes.

Abonnementskonzerte werden von dem Philadelphia Orchester jeden Dienstag-, Donnerstag-, und Samstagabend su wie Freitagnachmittag in der Academy of Music gegeben. Im Sommer gibt es eine Fünfwochenserie von Konzerten auf der Freilichtbühne des Robin Hood Dell im Fairmount Park. Oft werden einzelne Veranstaltungen von etwa 30 000 Menschen besucht.

La Orchesta de Philadelphia da varios conciertos de abono en la Academia de Música las noches de martes, jueves, y sábado y también por las tardes de viernes. En el verano, se ofrece una serie de conciertos de cinco semanas al aire libre en Robin Hood Dell que está situado en Fairmount Park a donde asisten más de 30 mil aficionados de la música.

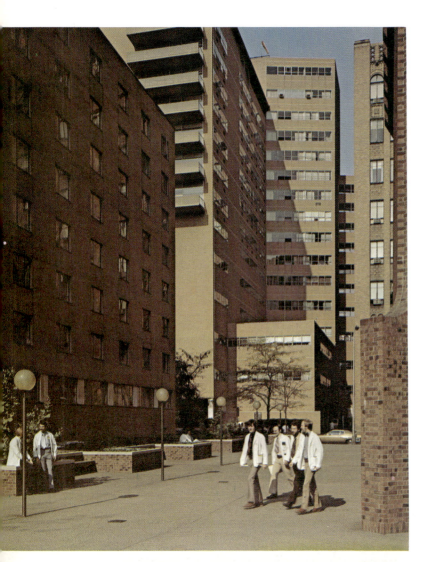

With forty accredited colleges and universities located in the city and suburbs, Philadelphia life is richly flavored with campus and classroom activity. Four medical schools are among the institutions here, three schools of law and schools of music, art, religion, business and science. Future doctors are changing classes at Thomas Jefferson University medical college; a Drexel University student rests in front of one of that school's new buildings; and University of Pennsylvania students cross a quadrangle.

Quarante "colleges" et universités se situent dans la région de Philadelphie y comprises quatre facultés de médecine, trois facultés de droit, et d'autres de musique, de beaux arts, de religion, de commerce, et de science.

Vierzig Colleges und Universitäten befinden sich in der Stadt und der Umgebung; unter ihnen sind vier Hochschulen für Medizin, drei für das Jurastudium wie auch Hochschulen für Musik, Kunst, Religion, Wirtschafts- und Naturwissenschaften.

Unos cuarenta acreditados institutos y universidades están situados dentro y cerca de Philadelphia, incluyendo cuatro facultades de medicina, tres de leyes y facultades de música, arte, religión, negocios y ciencias.

Three colleges founded by the Quakers—Bryn Mawr, Haverford and Swarthmore—are located within a few miles of each other in Philadelphia suburban communities which carry their names. Haverford College was established in 1833 for men, and Bryn Mawr in 1880 for women. Swarthmore College was founded in 1864 and has always been co-educational. At Bryn Mawr, the English-style Martha Carey Thomas Building is named in honor of the remarkable woman who was the college's first dean and later its president. On the Swarthmore campus, a long walk beneath arching oak trees leads uphill to Parrish Hall, the main administration building.

Trois "colleges" fondés par les Quakers, Bryn Mawr, Haverford, et Swarthmore se trouvent à quelques miles l'un de l'autre dans la banlieu de Philadelphie. Bryn Mawr est un "college" de femmes; Haverford est pour hommes et Swarthmore est mixte.

Drei Colleges—Bryn Mawr, Haverford und Swarthmore—wurden von den Quäkern gegründet. Sie liegen in der Philadelphia Vorstadt einige Meilen von einander entfernt. Bryn Mawr ist ein College für Studentinnen, Haverford für Studenten; Swarthmore wird von beiden besucht.

Tres "Colleges" fundados por los cuáqueros—Bryn Mawr, Haverford, y Swarthmore—están situados unas pocas millas de sí mismos en los arrabales de Philadelphia. Bryn Mawr es un "college" de mujeres; Haverford para los hombres, y Swarthmore admite los dos sexos.

Although Philadelphia is situated 90 miles from the ocean, it is one of the world's major seaports. The broad and deep Delaware River provides a safe and secure harbor, enabling seagoing vessels to come directly within the city's boundaries and dock within a mile of City Hall. The volume of shipping in and out of the Port of Philadelphia exceeds that of London.

Modern apartment towers now overlook Penn's Landing, the section of the waterfront where Penn and his Quaker settlers first came ashore.

Quoique Philadelphie se trouve à 90 miles de l'océan, le large et profond fleuve Delaware pourvoit un port sûr qui permet aux long-courriers d'entrer dans la ville-même, à un mile de l'Hôtel de Ville. Des immeubles modernes donnent sur la partie des quais qui s'appellent "Penn's Landing" à cause de son histoire.

Obwohl Philadelphia 90 Meilen vom Ozean entfernt gelegen ist, hat die Stadt dennoch einen Hafen für Ozeandampfer, da der Delaware breit und tief genug ist, um den Schiffen die Einfahrt zu ermöglichen, so dass sie nur eine Meile vom Stadtzentrum entfernt anlegen können. Moderne Hochhäuser schauen auf das Hafenviertel herab, das "Penn's Landing" genannt wird.

Aunque Philadelphia está situada 90 millas del océano, el ancho y profundo río Delaware provee un puerto seguro que facilita la entrada en dique de los barcos desde una milla del Ayuntamiento. Ahora las torres de unos apartamentos dominan la sección de la marina que, a causa de su pasada historia se llama "Penn's Landing."

Because of its excellent port facilities, Philadelphia has attracted many diverse industries. Oil refining, chemical manufacturing and steelmaking have all clustered nearby to take advantage of water transportation, and over the years, coal and grain have been important items of export through the port. Now, however, Philadelphia's waterfront bustles with another kind of activity—container shipping. Widespread truck transportation brings giant pre-packed containers the size of truck trailers directly to shipside. Giant cranes swing them into the hold or onto the deck of a container ship in minutes. Ship turn-around time is only a matter of a day or so.

Le transport par camion largement répandu a causé une révolution dans la mise à bord des conteneurs. On conduit directement aux quais des conteneurs préconditionnés aussi grands qu'une remorque de camion. Des grues géantes les hissent à bord en quelques minutes et le temps de rotation est réduit à un jour ou à peu près.

Der LKW-Transport hat den Hafenbetrieb revolutioniert und das sogennante "Container Shipping" eingeführt. Vorgepackte Kontainer, so gross wie ein LWK-Anhänger, werden an das Schiff gebracht. Innerhalb von Minuten heben riesige Kräne sie an Bord, und der Aufenthalt des Schiffes im Hafen wird dadurch auf einen Tag verkürzt.

El transporte difuso de camiones ha efectuado una revolución en la actividad del puerto—el embarque de envases. Se llevan directamente al lado de los barcos unos envases ya empaquetados que son tan grandes como un wagón de camión.

Philadelphia's advantages as a port include the close and easy links between river, highway and rail transportation. Interstate Highway 95 (north and south) and the Pennsylvania Turnpike (east and west) are both at the doorstep of the waterfront and the vast industrial area of northeast Philadelphia.

Port activity extends well beyond the boundaries of the city itself. Nearby on the river are Camden, Trenton and Paulsboro, New Jersey; Chester and Marcus Hook, Pennsylvania; and Wilmington, Delaware. Shipping men call the entire area "Ameriport."

Philadelphie jouit d'une correspondence serrée et facile entre les transports de fleuve, de route, et de chemin de fer. L'activité du port dépasse de beaucoup les bornes de la ville, depuis Trenton, New Jersey jusqu'à Wilmington, Delaware. Les expéditeurs appellent la région entière, "Ameriport."

In Philadelphia besteht eine enge Verbindung zwischen Fluss-, Strasse- und Bahntransport. Der Hafenverkehr erstreckt sich weit über die Grenzen der Stadt— von Trenton, New Jersey bis nach Wilmington, Delaware. Die Schiffer und Hafenarbeiter nennen die ganze Gegend "Ameriport."

Philadelphia tiene buenos enlaces de transporte entre los ríos, las carreteras y los ferrocarriles. Las actividades del puerto se extienden más allá de los límites de la misma ciudad—desde Trenton, New Jersey hasta Wilmington, Delaware. Los mercaderes de barcos llaman toda la área "Ameriport."

Philadelphia's big event on New Year's Day is the Mummers' Parade. Thousands take part in it, and hundreds of thousands come in family groups to watch. Since 1901, it has been a genuine folk festival, still entirely free of commercial floats and advertising.

The tradition is kept alive by scores of neighborhood clubs whose members devote much of the year to planning and working on theme ideas and costumes for the comic, fancy dress or string band divisions of the parade. On New Year's Day, Broad Street is closed to traffic. The parade begins at eight in the morning. It is usually well after dark before the last units reach the judges' stand at City Hall.

The string bands—unique Philadelphia organizations—are always the favorites in their elaborately feathered costumes. There is never a trumpet or a tuba. Banjos and violins are plentiful. And even in the coldest weather, many a sturdy Mummer walks five miles along Broad Street vigorously playing a bass fiddle strapped over his shoulder.

Une tradition de Philadelphie est le défilé des "Mummers" le Jour de l'An, un véritable festival folklorique sans aucune sorte de publicité commerciale. Les clubs des quartiers de la ville y envoient des milliers de participants qui défilent toute la journée. Ce qui est unique à Philadelphie ce sont les "Mummers," des orchestres à cordes qui sont toujours très appréciés.

Eine Tradition Philadelphias ist die Neujahrsparade der sogennanten Mummer, ein wahres Volksfest, vollkommen frei von jeglichem Handelsgeist. Viele Tausend Mitglieder der verschiedenen Vereine der Umgebung marschieren mit; die Parade dauert den ganzen Tag. Philadelphias einzigartige Streichorchester sind sehr beliebt.

Una de las más antiguas tradiciones de Philadelphia es la parada de bandas "Mummers" del primero de Año, una auténtica fiesta folklórica libre de anuncios y comerciales. Los miles de participantes vienen de los clubes de varios barrios de la ciudad, y el desfile continúa todo el día. Una característica destacada es la serie de bandas de cuerdas.

Progress Plaza at Broad and Jefferson Streets is the prototype of minority-owned and minority-managed shopping centers rising throughout this country and abroad as ventures of Zion Investment Associates, founded by Dr. Leon H. Sullivan, pastor of Philadelphia's Zion Baptist Church. Members of his congregation pay $10 a month for 36 months to buy shares. They are aided by business and by the community.

Progress Plaza est un centre commercial dont les propriétaires et les directeurs sont d'une des minorités nationales. C'est le prototype des centres pareils que sont en train de s'établir partout aux Etats-Unis. La société qui possède ce centre-ci s'appelle Zion Investment Associates, fondée par le pasteur de Zion Baptist Church et lancée par ses paroissiens, aidés par certains hommes d'affaire et d'autres individus de la ville.

Progress Plaza gehört der schwarzen Minorität, die auch das Shopping Center verwaltet. Es ist ein Prototyp für ähnliche Zentren, die überall in den Vereinigten Staaten im Entstehen sind. Es gehört der Zion Investment Associates, die vom Pastor der Zion Baptist Church gegründet wurde. Die Geldmittel wurden von den Mitgliedern seiner Gemeinde so wie von Geschäftsleuten und der Bevölkerung des umliegenden Bezirks zur Verfügung gestellt.

Progress Plaza es un centro de compras de reventa cuyos dueños son un grupo de minorías que dirigen todo y es un prototipo de otros semejantes centros que están apareciendo por los Estados Unidos. Los dueños son los Asociados Zion Investment, fundado por el pastor de la iglesia Zion Baptist y consolidado por los miembros de su congregación ayudado por la comunidad y hombres de negocios.

An out of the ordinary shopping experience in downtown Philadelphia is a visit to the colorful sidewalk market on South Ninth Street.

Un expérience intéressante dans Philadelphie est une promenade au marché en plein air qui longe les trottoirs de la rue 9.

Ein interessantes Einkaufserlebnis in Philadelphia ist der Bürgersteigmarkt in der South Ninthstrasse.

Una experiencia interesante en el centro de la ciudad es ir de compras en el mercado al aire libre en la calle South Ninth.

Philadelphia's sports complex along South Broad Street is one of the best in the nation. The larger oval is Veterans' Stadium, home of the Phillies baseball team and the green-shirted Eagles of the National Football League. Just beyond is the Spectrum, the indoor arena where the Flyers play hockey and the Seventy-Sixers play basketball. Still further south is John F. Kennedy Stadium with a capacity of more than 100,000. This is where one of the country's major sports events, the Army-Navy football game, is played.

Les trois plus grandes installations de sports sont voisines dans "South" Philadelphie. La plus proche du centre est Veterans' Stadium où se jouent le baseball et le football professionels; un peu plus loin se trouve le Spectrum, stade fermé pour le hockey et le basketball. Encore plus loin se trouve John F. Kennedy Stadium qui a plus de 100.000 places.

Die drei grossen städtischen Sportstadien liegen alle in South Philadelphia. Im vordergrund befindet sich das Veterans' Stadium, wo Berufsspiele der Baseball- und Footballmanschaften stattfinden. Dahinter liegt das Spectrum, eine Hockey- und Basketballspielhalle. Im Hintergrund sieht man das John F. Kennedy Stadium, das über 100 000 Sitzplätze hat.

Muy juntas en el Sur de Philadelphia están las tres más importantes facilidades de deportes de la ciudad. En el primer plano es Veterans' Stadium, casa de los equipos profesionales de baseball y football. Más allá es el Spectrum, un coliseo interior para hockey y basketball. En el fondo es John F. Kennedy Stadium, que tiene la capacidad de albergar a 100,000 espectadores.

An unusual aspect of Philadelphia's remarkable renewal program is a requirement of the Redevelopment Authority that one percent of the cost of new construction projects be invested in works of art to be permanently displayed at the site. This is Bingham Court, Third and Spruce Streets, where new townhouses have been designed as links between rows of Eighteenth Century homes and high-rise apartments at the waterfront.

Ces maisons de Bingham Court ont été construites dans le but de servir de liason entre les maisons style 18ème siècle et les grands immeubles modernes. Un pour-cent des frais des modernisations publiques à Philadelphie doit être placé dans des oeuvres d'art destinées à être exposées définitivement sur les lieux des nouveaux édifices.

Diese neuen Townhouses in Bingham Court sollen eine Verbindung zwischen den Häusern aus dem 18. Jahrhundert und den Hochhäusern herstellen. Ein Prozent der mit neuen Projekten verbundenen Kosten müssen in Kunstwerken investiert werden, die an dieser Stelle ihren Platz finden.

Estas nuevas casas de ciudad en Bingham Court están planeadas como eslabón entre las casas del siglo diez y ocho y los apartamentos altos y modernos. Uno por ciento del precio de los nuevos proyectos de renovación en Philadelphia tiene que ser invertido en las obras de arte que se exhiben permanentemente en este lugar.

At Christmastime, shoppers arrange their schedules to be at the John Wanamaker store at least once at show time. In the store's grand court, high above the large bronze eagle, which is Wanamaker's symbol, a holiday fantasy is presented with music, colored lights, and illuminated fountains.

A Noël, le spectacle dans la Grande Cour du magasin John Wanamaker attire du monde plusieurs fois par jour.

In der Weihnachtszeit zieht die Weihnachtsvorstellung in der Haupthalle des Kaufhauses John Wanamaker viele Besucher mehrere Male am Tage an.

Durante la Navidad, el espectáculo navideño en el Patio Central del almacén John Wanamakers atrae muchos compradores varias veces al día.

"Faire Mount"- The Great Park

In 1682, the official surveyor preparing a plan of Philadelphia, designated a little hill on the east bank of the Schuylkill, "Faire Mount." William Penn originally intended to build his home there. Later, it was the site of the reservoir for the municipal waterworks. Today, the Philadelphia Museum of Art is located there. And beyond it, stretching for miles along both sides of the river, is Philadelphia's un-equalled, city-owned Fairmount Park.

The Park is within a few minutes walk or ride from residential neighborhoods on all sides and, by way of the Parkway, from the center of the downtown district. On summer week-ends and holidays, as many as half a million Philadelphians a day find open space, beauty, fresh air and recreation within its boundaries.

Sur un vieux plan de Philadelphie l'arpenteur désigna une petite colline sous le nom "Faire Mount." Aujourd'hui, Fairmount est le parc municipal inégalé de 2.000 hectares qui s'étend en plein milieu de la ville. Souvent en été il peut y avoir jusqu'à un demi million de Philadelphiens qui cherchent le plein air, la beauté et le divertissment sur ses terrains.

Auf einer frühen Karte von Philadelphia hatten die Landmesser einen kleinen Hügel "Faire Mount" genannt. Heute ist Fairmount der Name des grossangelegten Stadtparks, der sich über 4 000 Morgen Land durch die Stadt erstreckt. Während der Sommertage kommt oft eine halbe Million Stadtbewohner in die Parkanlagen, wo sie den freien Raum, die Schönheit der Natur und die Möglichkeiten eines fröhlichen Zeitvertreibs geniessen.

En uno de los primeros planes de Philadelphia, el agrimensor llamó una colina pequeña "Faire Mount." Hoy día, Fairmount es el nombre de un parque, sin rival y poseído municipalmente de 4 mil acres que se extienden por el interior de la ciudad. En los días estivales medio millón de habitantes de Philadelphia gozan del espacio libre, la hermosura y el recreo dentro de sus límites.

Games of rugby and cricket are played regularly in Fairmount Park along with baseball, football and soccer. Sailboats appear on the river almost the entire year around, and grassy banks provide a refuge for wildlife. Miles of trails are laid out for riding bicycles or horses, for jogging and for hiking; but of all park activities, perhaps family picnicking is the most popular.

The Philadelphia Zoo, the oldest in the nation and one of the best, has occupied a corner of the Park for a century.

Generations of Philadelphians have been proud of the Park, giving or bequeathing gardens, walkways, groves of trees and statuary to enhance it. One notable organization, The Fairmount Park Art Association, exists entirely for the purpose of providing works of art to decorate the Park.

Le Fairmount Park fournit toutes sortes de divertissements pour les Philadelphiens aussi bien qu'un lieu de refuge pour le gibier d'eau. Ses autres installations comprennent un excellent jardin zoologique, un théâtre d'été sous chapiteau, et un amphithéâtre pour les concerts. On peut voir des bateaux sur la rivière presque toute l'année.

Fairmount Park bietet den Stadtbewohnern viele Erholungsmöglichkeiten. Auch die Wildvögel finden Schutz. Im Park finden wir auch einen zoologischen Garten, ein Sommertheater und eine Freilichtbühne. Boote sieht man fast das ganze Jahr auf dem Fluss.

Fairmount Park provee unos recreos de muchas clases por los habitantes de Philadelphia tanto como un refugio por los aves salvajes. Sus facilidades incluyen un excelente jardín zoológico, un teatro de verano y un auditorio al aire libre. Se ven unos barcos en el río por casi todo el año.

"The Schuylkill Navy," based along Boathouse Row in Fairmount Park, is a long-established institution. Philadelphia oarsmen have won national and international honors over the years, and the Schuylkill course has been the scene of more championship rowing events than any other in the country.

Many high schools in the Philadelphia area have crews and participate in rowing races along with the colleges and universities. Even more active are the amateur clubs—women's and men's—whose members can be seen on the river in eights, fours, doubles and singles from early morning to near sundown in the summer season.

The banks of the Schuylkill take on a country fair atmosphere on regatta days when there are races sweeping down the river all day long.

Le Schuylkill, rivière des courses d'aviron, a été le lieu de plus de championnats d'aviron qu'aucun autre lieu dans tout le pays. Bien des écoles et universités des environs de Philadelphie en ont des équipes et les mettent en compétition dans les régates sur le Schuylkill. Les jours de course les rives de la rivière ressemblent à une foire de campagne.

Auf dem Abschnitt des Schuykills, der durch Fairmount Park fliesst, wurden mehr Ruderwettbewerbe veranstaltet als irgendwo anders im Land. Viele High Schools und Colleges aus Philadelphia und Umgebung haben ihre eigenen Ruderbootmanschaften, die an der Schuykillregatta teilnehmen. Während dieser Tage herrscht an den Ufern des Flusses eine regelrechte Jahrmarktatmosphäre.

El hipódromo Schuylkill ha sido el lugar de la escena de los más exitosos campionatos del deporte de las regatas. Muchas escuelas y universidades de Philadelphia tienen equipos que se rivalizan en regatas en el Schuylkill. Durante los días de regata, las orillas del río tienen semejanza con una feria del campo.

The northernmost section of Fairmount Park branches from the Schuylkill and extends some five miles through the lovely valley of a creek with an Indian name, Wissahickon. Since William Penn's time, poets, painters and photographers have admired the natural beauty of the Wissahickon with its rushing water and rocky walls like a miniature canyon. Philadelphia bridge designers, with equal appreciation, have spanned the valley without spoiling its charm. Along much of the Wissahickon, automobiles are banned and the paths are reserved for walking.

Une des plus charmantes parties du Fairmount Park c'est la vallée qui suit le cours d'un ruisseau qui a un nom indien, Wissahickon. Pour la plupart les automobiles sont interdites le long du Wissahickon et le sentiers sont réservés pour les piétons.

Einer der schönsten Teile des Fairmount Parks ist das Tal, durch das ein Bach mit dem indianischen Namen Wissahickon fliesst. Dieses Tal ist teilweise für den Autoverkehr gesperrt; es gibt dort viele Pfade für Spaziergänger.

Una de las secciones más atractivas de Fairmount Park es el valle que sigue el camino de un riachuelo con un nombre indio, Wissahicken. Se prohibe el uso de automóviles por casi todo el Wissahicken, y las sendas están reservadas para los caminantes.

"... This day my country was confirmed to me under the great seal of England," William Penn wrote on January 5, 1681, " 'Tis a clear and just thing, and my God that has given it me through many difficulties will, I believe, bless and make it the seed of a nation ..."

Not quite a century later, the State House of Pennsylvania became the birthplace of the United States of America.

Le jour où le roi anglais lui accorda une province, William Penn écrivit qu'il la croyait le futur "germe d'une nation." Presqu'un siècle plus tard la Chambre de l'Etat de Pennsylvanie devint le berceau des Etats-Unis d'Amérique.

An dem Tage an dem William Penn die Provinz vom Britischen König geschenkt wurde, schrieb er, er glaube, sie werde "das Saatkorn der Nation" werden. Kaum ein Jahrhundert später wurde das State House von Pennsylvania die Geburtsstätte der Vereinigten Staaten von Amerika.

La dia que el tomada el concesión de su provincia del Rey Británico, William Penn escribienda que él creada que ello habra será "la semilla de la nación." A menos que un siglo luego, el edificio de la Camera Legislativa de Pensilvania llegó el suelo natal de los Estados Unidos.